LENIN–The Exile Returns

Lenin at the time of his arrest in 1895. This was the photograph on his police card.

LENIN
The Exile Returns

Kenneth F.
and
Heloise P. Mailloux

AUERBACH.
publishers

princeton
philadelphia
new york
london

Library of Congress Catalog Card Number: 74-163108
International Standard Book Number: 0-87769-091-X

First Printing

Printed in the United States of America

To
ELIZABETH MACKAY PIKE

Contents

Note

Until February 1918, Russia used the Julian (Old Style) calendar, which in the nineteenth century was 12 days and in the twentieth century 13 days behind the West's Gregorian calendar. We have retained the Julian dates here to avoid discrepancy with historical names. (By the Gregorian calendar, the February Revolution would be dated March; the April Days, May; and the October Revolution, November.)

At the outbreak of World War I, St. Petersburg was renamed Petrograd. (In the nationalistic spirit of those days, many place-names were Russianized.) But some of the revolutionaries quoted in these pages were Internationalists—that is, they hoped for worldwide revolution and disliked nationalism. They refused to use "Petrograd," and called the city "Petersburg." We have used "Petrograd" in the text except when quoting an Internationalist. Neither place-name exists any longer except in history; the city is now called Leningrad.

1. Background

Many men have dreamed of changing the world, and some have tried to make the dream come true. Few have succeeded as spectacularly as did Lenin, who saw in the Russian Revolution of 1917 the opportunity he had been waiting for—the opportunity to make Russia communistic. Not that Lenin made the revolution. It took hundreds of years of intolerable living conditions to do that. Russia had always had uprisings in which peasants and workers ran amok because life had pushed them beyond endurance. These uprisings were leaderless, aimless, and very violent. They solved no problems, and the rioters were usually subdued by very harsh methods. Ever since the Middle Ages, Russian rulers had maintained secret police and special troops to combat civil disorders.

It is not surprising that the peasants rioted. What is surprising is that they never revolted against the tsar. They believed that he was chosen by God to rule them, and that if he had only known of their plight, he would have helped them. The upper classes knew better, so it was from their group that the first social reformers came. The Decembrists* were a notable

---

* The members called themselves the Northern Society and the Southern Society, but after their December demonstration, they were always referred to as "Decembrists."

example. They were young army officers who had seen Europe while fighting Napoleon, and had returned to Russia determined to make their beloved country as modern as the West. Their aim was not so much philanthropic, to help the people, as it was patriotic, to make Russia a world power. They reasoned that Russia's archaic social structure was a terrible handicap.* When Nicholas I was proclaimed tsar in 1825, the officers saw a chance to force social reform. They were not thinking in terms of ultimatums or even of specific programs, but wanted to impress the tsar with such "new" ideas as freedom, equality, and limited monarchy. They told their men that Nicholas was a usurper, and that he had imprisoned his brother Constantine, the true heir. (Actually, Constantine had renounced the throne.) So, in December, 1825, the aroused soldiers followed their leaders into what was, in fact, a tiny revolution of the elite. The attackers surrendered at the first shots from Nicholas's defenders, and were sentenced harshly— five were hanged and 120 exiled to hard labor—but they became heroes to concerned young people, and inspired other well-born, well-educated, nationalistic youths to follow their example.

As revolutionaries multiplied, so did the machinery for suppressing them. Nicholas I empowered the Third Section (secret police) to investigate all education, communication, administration—even the fine arts—and to stamp out any hint of subversion anywhere. He also set up the "reptile press," journalists paid to promote the monarchy, the Orthodox Church, and Russian chauvinism. Later tsars employed similar means, which naturally widened the gulf between monarch and intellectual community.

* At the end of the French Revolution, an estimated 34,000,000 of Russia's 36,000,000 inhabitants were serfs. Of course serfdom was a complex structure, and there were serfs who owned other serfs. Some even owned great industries and the towns surrounding them. But for the most part serfdom was both oppressive and unproductive, and a great burden to the country.

In 1861 the serfs were emancipated, but for many emancipation brought increased misery. Those freed without enough land to live on had little choice but to petition to leave the village for the city. There, they had to compete in a market already glutted with unskilled labor. Living conditions were unspeakable, and laws enacted to protect workers were not enforced. Uprisings became more and more common, but still the workers did not denounce the tsar. They rioted, breaking and burning, but if they voiced a grievance, it was always specific and immediate: they had not been paid, or the meat had been rotten again, or a comrade had been killed by faulty factory equipment. They never blamed the government.

Many educated people did blame the government, and by the sixties and seventies the more revolutionary of them were trying to agitate among the common people. In 1874 the Pilgrimage to the People sent thousands of idealistic young intellectuals—mostly university students—into the countryside. For many of them, it was a disillusioning or bewildering experience. They had assumed that the peasants were good, openhearted, simple, and exploited. They discovered that the peasants were guileful and suspicious of strangers. The most suspicious turned the young people over to the police, and even the more tolerant peasants seemed to assume that this was merely some new upper-class fad, and no business of theirs. They were not at all ready to listen to revolutionary agitation.

Lenin was only four years old when the Pilgrimage to the People took place. He had been born on April 10, 1870, in Simbirsk. (He was not called Lenin then, of course, but was christened Vladimir Ilyich Ulyanov. Not until the 1900s did he begin using the name "Lenin," and even then he used other names as well. But since he used so many pseudonyms, it is less confusing to call him Lenin from the beginning.) He was the third child of Ilya Nikolaevich Ulyanov and Maria Alexandrovna Blank Ulyanova; later they would have four more children. (The brothers and sisters were Anna, born 1864; Alexander, 1866; Vladimir (Lenin), 1870; Olga, 1871; Nikolai, 1873 (he died shortly after birth); Dmitri, 1874; and Maria, 1878.)

The six brothers and sisters grew up in the provincial city of Simbirsk, on the Volga River. It was a shipping center, and many of its 30,000 inhabitants were boatmen of Asian descent. The Ulyanovs were not completely Great Russian either. Lenin's paternal grandmother had been a Kalmuck. The Kalmucks were Buddhists, and their Asian ancestors had left them a physical, as well as a religious heritage. Lenin and his father both had high cheek bones and oriental eyes. Lenin's mother, moreover, was half-German, and was also Lutheran at a time when any religion but Russian Orthodoxy was thought to be evidence of foreign influence and possible subversion.

Nevertheless, theirs was not a revolutionary household. The parents were upper middle class intellectuals. (American tourists who view the rooms of Lenin's childhood home now displayed in a museum often comment on their "un-Russian" quality, and see a resemblance to houses of the same period in, say, Concord, Massachusetts.) Lenin's father was director of the province's public schools. He built the system from 20 little schools to 434 primary schools and several excellent secondary schools, and his services earned him a title—the fourth in Peter the Great's table of 14 ranks, and therefore inheritable. (Young Lenin used it when he wanted to impress officialdom.)

They were a reading and writing family, and all the children excelled in school. At that time, the examination for graduation from public school was formidable. It was prepared secretly, given under conditions guaranteed to prevent cheating (and, incidentally, to heighten anxieties), and the middle class student's whole future rested on its outcome. It was the only door to a university education and a job. Candidates often had nervous breakdowns. But as their turns came, Alexander and Anna not only passed, but took first place among all local

The Ulyanov family in 1879, when Lenin was nine. He is seated at the far right.

candidates, winning the coveted gold medal. Each went on to a university.

When Lenin's turn came for the exams, the family was undergoing a terrible ordeal. In March, 1887, Alexander and Anna had been arrested with a group of St. Petersburg students who had plotted to assassinate the tsar. Anna had had no part in the plot, and was merely exiled to her grandfather's country estate, but Alexander was facing a death sentence. Their father had died the year before, but their mother was a resourceful woman. She rode a horse 60 miles in order to get a train to St. Petersburg, and tried every contact and entreaty to save Alexander. (Since the conspirators had never actually put their plan into operation, there was hope.) But Alexander insisted, for ideological reasons, on making a speech in court in which he condemned the tsarist regime and emphasized his revolutionary convictions. He was hanged on May 8, 1887. His mother was with him. "Take courage," she said. Lenin sat for his exams that same week, and upheld family tradition by winning the gold medal. He was already capable of controlling emotion when he felt that it conflicted with duty.

Very little is known about the ideals and desires of the boy who was to become Lenin, partly because early Soviet biographers built a personality cult around him, suppressing or distorting whatever facts conflicted with the picture they wanted to emerge. The Lenin worshipped by early Communists is not only too precocious to be true—they would have you believe he was born a revolutionary—but is also less complicated and interesting than he really was. There is no evidence to show that young Lenin shared his brother's revolutionary convictions. He seems to have been mystified by them, and he questioned Alexander's friends, as though trying to piece together what had happened to motivate his brother. And while Alexander's death caused him grief, it did not radicalize Lenin directly. It took the tsarist government's obsession with security to do that.

Lenin went off to Kazan University in the summer of 1887 to study law, as he had planned. Kazan was a provincial university, and not so radical as St. Petersburg or Moscow, but the government's intrusion into university affairs had resulted in making most students political activists, and protests were very common. When a demonstration occurred at Kazan in Decem-

Lenin at the age of 15.

ber* Lenin was expelled and exiled to his grandfather's estate in rural Kokushkino. He had not been a leader, instigator, or outstanding participant in the protest, but because of Alexander, his name was on the police lists, and he was treated as a revolutionary.

His first thoughts were of returning to the university as soon as possible, and his mother petitioned for that. But the Ministry of Education refused. Next, his mother petitioned the Ministry of the Interior for permission for Lenin to go abroad to study, but again the request was denied. He was left at loose ends, without a formal course of study, for the first time since he had learned to read. For the next three years, as his mother tried to get the authorities to readmit him to the university, Lenin read. He discovered the revolutionary writers almost at once, and later wrote that he had become a Marxist in January, 1889, converted by Marx's *Capital* and Plekhanov's *Our Disagreements*. While the police took note of their comings and goings—the family had been allowed to leave Kokushkino, and lived first in Kazan and then on a farm in Samara Province—Lenin lived a quiet uneventful life, and dreamed of overthrowing the government.

He also studied law, and in January, 1892, petitioned the Minister of Education for permission to take the bar examinations. (He signed himself "Nobleman Vladimir Ulyanov.") Permission was granted, but after passing the exams, Lenin found that he would have to clear his police record in order to practice without restrictions. He took the trouble to unsnarl the

* The trouble began in Moscow, when a student was sentenced to three years in a penal battalion for having slapped the face of the student inspector. (These inspectors were thought of as spies.) Moscow students went out in a body, and the university closed temporarily. Students at all universities called sympathetic protests; at Kazan the student inspector ordered them to disperse, and was predictably manhandled. Aroused, the students passed resolutions in typical Russian fashion, while the authorities arrested more than 100, shut down the university for two months, and expelled 45 students, including Lenin, outright.

red tape, thus qualifying for a profession he had no intention of pursuing. He was already determined to make a career of revolution.

For two and one-half years longer, Lenin lived like a country gentleman in Samara, arguing a very few unimportant cases. He was impatient to be in a radical center, but seems to have stayed in the country because his mother's health was not good. (Life had dealt her one stunning blow after another; the most recent was Olga's death, from typhoid.) Throughout his life, Lenin was very close to his family, never too busy to consider their problems, and never hesitant to call on them for help. While she lived, his mother supported him—ironically, from her generous widow's pension (1,200 gold rubles annually) from the tsarist government.

In late summer of 1893, the family left Samara. The others journeyed to Moscow, but Lenin headed for St. Petersburg to seek and join the radicals there.

2. The Professional Revolutionary

When Lenin arrived in St. Petersburg he was 23, and looked much as he would in middle age. He was short-legged and stocky, balding and bearded, a small, ordinary-looking man, except for his very dark, piercing eyes. He acted and dressed like a middle-class lawyer—or like a middle-class lawyer uninterested in clothes and small talk. He was quiet and polite except during political exchanges, when he became as noisy as he thought necessary. Throughout his life, his habit was to try to win his opponent first by friendly argument. This succeeded very often; he was an informed and persuasive speaker. But if it failed, and if winning the match seemed important, Lenin took the offensive, hurling charges, accusations, and insults. He didn't care whether or not he was accurate, so long as he confounded his opponent. Very few could stand up to one of Lenin's barrages, and he might have been dismissed as an unscrupulous name-caller early in his career if it had not been for his sincere obsession with the revolution. He was totally committed to his dream of a Marxist Russia, and his morality was tailored to fit the dream. As far as he was concerned, what benefitted Marxism was moral, and what hurt it was immoral. His opponents might doubt his judgment, but they never questioned his sincerity.

Lenin had one inexplicable character trait which everyone who writes of him tries to explain, but which is still a matter for conjecture; he distrusted his own class. His dislike of the bourgeois liberal intellectual amounted to hatred, and was accompanied by an equally unreasoning admiration for the peasantry. He thought that peasants were basically more honest and trustworthy than people on higher rungs of the social ladder. This bias stayed with him all his life; his trust in Stalin was, for example, colored by Stalin's peasant background.

When young Lenin arrived in St. Petersburg, it was the most important city in Russia. It was the government center, the intellectual center, and the industrial center. Russia at that time had a very small middle class and almost no proletariat. (The word "proletariat" implies that the worker is factory-oriented, without ties to the land. Nearly all of Russia's factory workers were peasants who would have preferred to work the land. In thousands of cases, their factory contracts specified that they might return to the village to plant and harvest.) The handful of true proletarians—second- and third-generation workers, without ties to the land—were in Moscow and St. Petersburg. Lenin, as a Marxist, depended on the proletariat to make the revolution, and so was eager to know as many of them as he could.

Many young agitators ran "Sunday schools" for workers—ostensibly, they were to teach the workers to read and write; actually, the agitators tried to acquaint them with Marx, or other revolutionary theorists. It was not illegal to read and discuss Marx. Because *Capital* had seemed so scholarly and abstruse the Russian censors had passed a translation of Volume I in 1872, five years after Marx published it. Marxism cannot be summed up accurately in a few words, but roughly, Marx believed that ownership of land had led early man to class distinctions, that the upper classes now exploited the lower classes, that the proletariat would one day rise up against its exploiters, and that capitalism would then be replaced by socialism, which would take from each according to his abilities, and give to each according to his needs. It was not a popular philosophy with Russian revolutionaries for several reasons. One was its concept that socialism would grow out of capitalism. Since Russia had not yet industrialized, this in effect meant that revolutionaries would have to wait until capitalism succeeded before expecting socialism. Similarly, Marx envisioned an overthrow by the proletariat, a class which hardly existed in Russia, where revolutionaries traditionally thought in terms of a peasant uprising. And Marxism was not attractive to the terrorists who joined revolutionary movements as an excuse for violence.

Indoctrination of the workers was slow work. They had so many specific physical problems that it was difficult to get them to consider abstract theories, and they had no reason to trust their young teachers. But the agitators had realized that they could use the government to destroy the government. If they encouraged the workers to strike for specific working demands, the government would overreact, and when the workers were treated like revolutionaries they would become revolutionaries. It was an eminently practical plan, and the tsarist government cooperated fully, with treatment of strikers so harsh that it made more converts to the revolutionary cause than years of reading Marx could have done. Two of Lenin's favorite sayings were, "The worse it is [for the common people], the better it is [for the revolution]," and "One who has been whipped is worth two who have not."

Lenin stayed in St. Petersburg for two years. He had joined a law firm, but hardly worked except at revolution. He had been accepted into a Marxist circle on the strength of his being Alexander's brother (Alexander was revered as a martyr), but once in he worked tirelessly and made a reputation of his own. In 1894 his first major political pamphlet, *What are "Friends of the People" and How They Fight Against the Social Democrats* was published. (Lenin was a Social Democrat, and the

Lenin at the age of 27.

pamphlet was an attack on the Narodniks, another party.) Like all of his work in years to come, it was polemical—that is, it set out to sell a point of view. Lenin never wrote objectively, weighing all the arguments impartially. Like a trial lawyer, he planned to win his case, and never introduced an argument against it unless he could refute it effectively. Lenin usually wrote propaganda rather than agitation—he had accepted Plekhanov's* distinction, which said that propaganda took many complicated ideas to a few, while agitation took a few simple ideas to many. Throughout his life, Lenin wrote primarily for professional revolutionaries, instructing them, trying to build a cohesive party. It is therefore risky to quote any single article of his as an illustration of his ideology. Often he wrote in furious rebuttal, because he saw in some new development a threat to the revolution. To judge any of his writings, it is necessary to consider what was being written by his contemporaries. All his articles are responses to world events, and he did not hesitate to oversimplify, distort, or contradict his own earlier writings in order to win a battle in the propaganda war.

In 1894 Lenin also met Nadezhda Konstantinovna Krupskaya. She was a girl of the upper class who had become a revolutionary, and like Lenin, was trying to educate workers in her views. (She disguised herself as a worker to investigate factory housing and to distribute agitation leaflets.) She and Lenin were soon seeing much of each other. For both, the revolution was the most important thing in life, and both were prepared to devote their lives to it.

Unlike most revolutionaries, Lenin was full of practical plans. The first step was to build the party, so the next year Lenin went abroad, officially for his health, but actually to meet Marxist exiles. He was taking the initiative in trying to unite them. He returned to St. Petersburg in the fall, and went on with his illegal publishing. In December, 1895, the police ar-

* Georgi V. Plekhanov pioneered in Russian socialism. He has even been called the father of Russian Marxism. Lenin said that Plekhanov's *Our Disagreements* was one of the books that converted him to Marxism.

rested 57 Marxists in St. Petersburg, including Lenin. It was nearly the whole local membership of the tiny party.

Lenin spent the next year in jail. It was the custom to arrest suspects and hold them until the investigation was completed before bringing them to trial. However, during that period, prisoners with contacts or influence were allowed food, books, and other comforts from outside, and Lenin was soon propagandizing from his cell. He wrote much of *Development of Russian Capitalism*, burdened his family and friends with constant errands and research, and kept himself fit with exercise.* At his trial, Lenin maintained that he had simply given legal advice to workers. He was sentenced to three years "free" exile in Siberia. Free exile meant that he could settle in an approved Siberian village and live as he chose within its boundaries.

Previously, the trip to Siberia had been an ordeal, but Lenin was fortunate in that a section of the Trans-Siberian Railroad had just been completed. He left in style, unguarded, in February, 1896. The trip was almost a vacation. At one point there was an anticipated stopover of several weeks. Not only had friends arranged for Lenin to stay with a wealthy sympathizer, but he had access to a fine private library in the area.†

---

* Lenin advocated exercise as part of party discipline. He said revolutionaries should be physically fit not only so that they could run if the need arose, but also because physical fitness made them less apt to develop the nervous disorders which were an occupational hazard of the revolutionary life. He himself often complained of "bad nerves," and hiked, climbed mountains, bicycled, ice skated, hunted, and fished as antidotes.

† Throughout his life, Lenin chose his temporary homes for their proximity to good libraries, and he became a familiar sight in many libraries. In the 1920s an elderly curator of the British Museum's library was asked if he remembered Lenin. He recalled no one of that name, but further questions revealed that he remembered a Mr. Ulyanov very well. He said, ". . . a very charming gentleman, short, and with a pointed beard. A very nicely-spoken gentleman. . . . Can you tell me . . . what became of him?" John Strachey, "The Great Awakening," *Encounter*, 5 (1961), p. 7. Lenin always obeyed library rules to the letter, and during his last illness reminded his sister that her son ought to return the book Lenin had borrowed.

Lenin's Siberian village was Shushenskoe, in Minusinsk District. It had a church, three taverns, and about 1,300 inhabitants. The climate was good, and Lenin made himself at home in a rented room and went on with his work. He wrote reams. His family fetched and sent and received and dispatched. Anna was virtually his secretary. By now all of the brothers and sisters were revolutionaries.

With Lenin's Siberian writings, his role as a reinterpreter of Marx becomes apparent. Russian Marxists tended to make a religion of their political beliefs, and to be fundamentalist in their observance. Anyone who changed a traditional Marxist concept was called a "revisionist"—always an insult. Lenin used the socialist vocabulary, and called only enemies "revisionists," but revise he did. He was a very practical man who thought in terms of programs, and then looked for ways to reconcile theory with the action he thought necessary. Justification could be found; Marx can be interpreted in many ways. Lenin combated criticism by blasting revisionists more vehemently than anyone else, and by insisting that his own plans did not constitute revision, but simply the right interpretation at last. He often quoted Engels, Marx's close friend and colleague, who had said that Marxism was not a dogma but a guide to action.

Lenin had been in exile one year when Krupskaya—as she is usually called by Communists—was also exiled. She petitioned to join him, but the authorities would allow it only if they married. Krupskaya traveled to Shushenskoe with her mother, and arrived when Lenin was out hunting. She wrote,

> At last Vladimir Ilyich returned from the hunt. He was surprised to see a light in his room. The landlord said . . . [that another exile] had come in drunk and had thrown all his books about. Ilyich ran up the steps. Just then I came out onto the porch and we met. We had a good long talk that night.*

* Nadezhda Konstantinovna Krupskaya, *Reminiscences of Lenin* (Moscow: Foreign Languages Publishing House, 1959), p. 32. Reprinted by permission of International Publishers Co., Inc.

Lenin had to wait for identification papers to arrive before he could get a marriage license, but as soon as they had unsnarled the red tape, he and Krupskaya were married. Considering that theirs was virtually a government-ordered marriage, they were a very compatible couple. Krupskaya was as involved in the revolution as Lenin, and a great help to him.

Lenin had decided while in St. Petersburg that his first task would be to unite the scattered Marxists by systematic daily effort. Now he realized that to avoid arrest he would have to live outside Russia. So when his term of exile ended, in February, 1900, he moved to the frontier town of Pskov. (Krupskaya had to stay in Siberia for one more year.) That summer he was allowed to go abroad, and he traveled, raising funds for the journal which he hoped would vitalize the party. The first issue appeared in Stuttgart, Germany in December, 1900. He had named it *Iskra* ("The Spark"), from a familiar Decembrist poem: "Out of this spark will come a conflagration"—the conflagration was to be international revolution. It was a professional journal, propaganda to consolidate party members, to teach the teachers, and to raise morale by binding isolated Marxists to the group. Its initial editors included veterans of the 1870s as well as younger leaders.

During the next few years, Lenin moved several times, either for convenience or because he felt that the Russian secret police were too close. He was very poor, but too busy to care. In February, 1901, the month before Krupskaya rejoined him, Lenin wrote his mother from Munich that it was so cold he was wearing two suits—he did not have an overcoat.

In March, 1902, *What Is to Be Done?* was published. It was signed "Lenin," and from then on, "Lenin" was his most familiar revolutionary name. It was a handbook of revolutionary tactics for Russian Marxists, but its ideas were a complete departure from established Marxist traditions. It advocated leadership by a small, select, secret organization of professional revolutionaries—small for unity and ease of communication; select, because only full-time professionals were adequate to the job,

Krupskaya in her late twenties.

and because it would be harder for the police to infiltrate; and secret, so that if ordinary members were arrested, they could not betray the whole leadership. Moreover, such an organization would lessen dissension. Marxism appeals to different types for very different reasons, and is descriptive, rather than prescriptive. That is, Marx described what he thought had happened and what he thought would happen, without indicating practical procedures for speeding up the process. He did not explain how the new socialism would function; that is, how the proletarian administration would work. Therefore, when his revolutionary followers were faced with practical decisions, there tended to be many opinions on how to cope without being false to Marx. The membership was exhausting its energies in argument. The leadership of professional revolutionaries, properly prepared, would prevent many such quarrels. Lenin was convinced that it was better to lose some members outright than to try to work with a party torn by internal dissension.

Lenin took his convictions to the Second Party Congress,* held in July and August, 1903. (It began in Brussels, but when the Belgian police seemed too interested, it moved to London.) Lenin's ideas received more (*bolshe*) votes and his opponents', fewer (*menshe*). The two names, Bolshevik and Menshevik became labels for the opposing factions, even though the Mensheviks soon outnumbered the Bolsheviks. The Congress voted to make *What Is to Be Done?* the official handbook of the party. However, it was clear to Lenin's opponents that the system it

---

* The first Russian Social Democratic Workers Party Congress had been held in Minsk in March, 1898, while Lenin was in Siberia. No one of first importance had attended; most were in exile. But the tiny gathering had adopted a name, discussed the possibilities of an all-Russian newspaper, and declared basic Marxist goals: immediately, a constitution, a freely elected parliament, freedom of speech and of the press, and, ultimately, common ownership of all means of production, including the land. When the delegates started home, most were arrested. At that time, arrests and quarrels within the party threatened to destroy even the German Social Democratic party, which was far stronger.

outlined needed a single leader, and while none who knew him accused him of personal ambition, there were many who from this time feared that Lenin would one day be dictator.

He left the congress the leader of the Bolsheviks; from this time on, Bolsheviks and Mensheviks were virtually separate parties. Lenin's impatience with the Mensheviks amounted to an obsession. Maria Essen, a girl who lived with the Ulyanovs for a time, recalled that on an outing in 1904, they climbed a Swiss peak and the view from the top was magnificent. She was overcome by its grandeur, and assumed Lenin was too. But when he broke the silence, what he said was, "The Mensheviks really mess things up."

3. Rehearsal for Revolution

In 1904 Lenin's dreams were pushed closer to reality by the Japanese. They attacked the Russian naval base at Port Arthur in January, and invaded Korea and Manchuria. Unprepared, inefficient, riddled with graft, Russia hadn't a chance in the war that followed. Lenin was delighted. He wrote, "It is the autocratic regime and not the Russian people that has suffered ignoble defeat. . . . The capitulation of Port Arthur is the prologue to the capitulation of tsardom."* Moreover, the war worsened living conditions in Russia to the point where people were sure to riot. Inflation, food shortages, and profiteering guaranteed it. When hunger came, violence followed.

The scene was set for revolution, but the people still supported tsardom. On Sunday, January 9, 1905, 200,000 workers, led by an Orthodox priest named Father Gapon, approached the Winter Palace to petition the tsar for help. They went peaceably and hopefully, carrying icons and portraits of the tsar, and singing patriotic songs. When he heard of their coming, Tsar Nicholas II went to his summer palace, leaving behind Cossacks who fired on the petitioners. In spite of instant dispersal, sev-

* V. I. Lenin, *Collected Works,* 4th ed., 45 vols. (Moscow: Foreign Languages Publishing House, vols. 1–19; Progress Publishers, vols. 20–45; 1960–1970) 8:53.

eral hundred people were killed or wounded. (Lenin wrote that
the government recorded 96 dead and 330 wounded, but the
newspapers estimated the casualties at 4,600.) "Bloody Sunday" made radicals of many workers, and launched paralyzing
general strikes.

It was a time when one strong convinced leader might have
made a true revolution, but such a leader was not forthcoming.
Lenin, in Geneva, tried to spur the Bolsheviks by mail, and to
advocate a program that a tiny group could perform—he knew
too well how small and weak the party was. He wrote that
Bolsheviks should form themselves into squads, armed with
whatever they could manage, and wage a kind of guerrilla warfare from ambush. He cautioned against terror for its own sake,
and urged that every foray have a goal, whether it was the
liberation of prisoners, the assassination of officials, or the
destruction of "enemy" property. But the Marxists in Russia
did relatively little. The Bolsheviks were still too weak, and
the Mensheviks were not only disorganized, but pacifistic. They
were convinced that capitalism would have to precede socialism,
so that it was "not their turn." When the proletariat rose up
and led the way, they would follow.

Without a leader, the Revolution of 1905 proceeded through
a series of isolated uprisings. There was the *Potemkin* mutiny
in June. Sailors aboard the *Potemkin* protested against eating
wormy meat, and their officers ordered them shot. The firing
squad refused, and instead the whole crew mutinied, raising the
red flag.* Other sailors of the squadron refused to fire on the
mutinous ship—conditions throughout the Black Sea Fleet were
intolerable—and in some cases they also mutinied. But like the
factory workers, the sailors were rioting, rather than revolting.
They were caught up in random violence, striking out without
a plan.

Many early uprisings are reported as political when they

*The red flag was a traditional symbol of revolution, dating back to
the French Revolution.

A Social Democratic cartoon of social classes in 1900.

were not. The police and government called them revolutionary revolts because they were always looking for subversion. The factory owners, or other authorities, called them revolts because they liked to pretend that their workers/soldiers/sailors would be content if only the agitators would leave them alone. The agitators called them revolts because part of the revolutionary strategy was to pretend to have far more than their real influence; they "took credit" for many uprisings with which they had had no connection.

But the workers had begun to organize. Fall brought the first Soviet, the Petrograd Soviet of Workers' Deputies. (Actually, "soviet" is a transliteration of the Russian word that means "council," and there were tsarist soviets. But this was the first council of delegates from workers' groups, an outgrowth of the strike committees. In revolutionary Russia, when the people yelled "All power to the Soviet," it was this sort of soviet they had in mind.) The first chairman of the Soviet was arrested and sent to Siberia on November 26. He was replaced by a committee of three, including Trotsky.* This brilliant, complex man was not a Bolshevik, but he had already contributed to Lenin's *Iskra*, and had become well acquainted with the Ulyanovs in London. He had returned to Russia in February, 1905, and by October was as much of a leader as the revolution had, but he lacked an organization—he hadn't even party apparatus to work with.

The demonstrations went by fits and starts. In October, the country was frozen by a general strike. It started over railroad workers' pension rights, but soon became political, and the telephone and telegraph workers joined in. Transportation and

---

* He was born Lev Davidovich Bronstein, in 1879, the son of rich peasants, and a natural rebel. He rebelled against his parents' values and his provincial unbringing, and finally against his government. When his revolutionary activities got him jailed and then exiled to Siberia, he escaped, "borrowing" the name of the head warden in the Odessa jail where he had been imprisoned—Leon Trotsky. He kept the name and made it famous.

communications ceased, and people of all backgrounds struck in sympathy. Peasants rampaged through the countryside, and finally sent delegates to Moscow to organize a peasants' union. All over Russia, city councils disbanded in favor of workers' soviets. By the end of November, they represented about 200,000 workers. (Membership covered 147 factories, 34 workshops, and 16 unions.) So far, the soviets were more like fraternal organizations than legislatures; they voted to support or censure governmental decisions, but had no practical authority. For example, a soviet repudiated the tsar's debts, but since it had absolutely nothing to say in the matter, it was merely a gesture.

During the 1905 revolution most groups which voiced political aims had modest hopes, by democratic standards. They wanted a constituent assembly and basic civil liberties. The tsar's advisers pleaded with him to grant these requests, not because they were solicitous of the downtrodden, but because anyone of any intelligence could see that revolution would come if change did not. Nicholas finally issued the Manifesto of October 17, 1905. It granted freedom of speech, assembly, and union, and stipulated that the State Duma (a kind of representative legislature which many liberals had been trying to get the tsar to allow) would have the final word on whether or not a law would be passed.

Until the October Manifesto, no political party had been legal in Russia, although antitsarist groups had existed underground. Now that the manifesto legalized party organization, the left came into the open, and the right set up its own parties. Many groups emerged. Roughly from right to left, they included:

1. The Union of the Russian People (the Black Hundreds). These were radical rightists. They upheld the autocracy and Orthodoxy, and were chauvinists. They were also terrorists, striking at socialists and minority groups, especially Jews. Their prejudices, including antiintellectualism, mirrored those

of Nicholas II, who was an honorary member and patronized the party. (It received funds from the secret police.) The regular membership came mostly from the lower middle class and the clergy.*

2. The Octobrists. These were usually upper class or upper middle class people who had been critical of the autocracy, but felt that the provisions of the October Manifesto, if carried out, would be concessions enough.

3. Constitutional Democrats (Kadets). Members were usually from the same classes as the Octobrists, but the Kadets were slightly to the left, with demands for a parliament, a constitutional monarchy, and forced sale of land to the peasants.

4. The Trudoviki (Labor Group). Like the Octobrists and Kadets, these were for the most part liberal intellectuals, but stood still further to the left on the land question. However, they were not socialists or revolutionaries.

5. Socialist Revolutionaries (SRs). An outgrowth of the old Populists and Narodniks, the SRs had existed underground for a long time, and were by far the largest revolutionary party, but lacked a program and an agreed objective. SR members ranged from those who would have been content to legislate within the autocracy to those who were terrorists and/or anarchists. The peasants were not politically inclined at this time, but insofar as they could be said to belong to a party, they were SRs. Russian peasants were very conservative and as prejudice-ridden as the Black Hundreds, which further complicated the party's activities.

6. Social Democrats (SDs). This was Lenin's party, already split into Menshevik and Bolshevik factions. All SDs believed in worker-led socialism, with Marx as the prophet, but they varied in their interpretation of Marx's teaching. The Mensheviks were closer to the original Marx; they wanted the middle class to establish a democracy in which the proletariat would

---

* Lenin's instructions from Geneva included retaliation against the Black Hundreds. He was not subtle: "Beat them up, kill them, and blow up their staff headquarters."

be able to work for true socialism. Lenin's Bolshevism was more Lenin than Marx; it was tailored to the problems of Russia, whereas Marxism had been formed around those of nineteenth-century Europe. Lenin linked the proletarian revolution with the peasant rather than with the bourgeoisie, and he intended to skip capitalism entirely.

After the October Manifesto, the Soviet demanded amnesty for political exiles, the evacuation of the army from Petrograd, and a people's militia. The tsar granted the amnesty, making it safe for Lenin to return. In November, he and Krupskaya arrived in Russia. He tried to rally the Bolsheviks, and advocated armed uprisings, but it was too late. The revolution had run out of steam. Now the revolutionaries argued among themselves. Most Mensheviks naturally advocated sweeping governmental reforms, and Lenin was furious. He had always warned that if the proletariat were given rights and comforts it would strive to become middle class, as it was doing in the West. He wanted conditions to get worse, not better, so that the people would revolt. Once they had, the new (Marxist) government which would result could see that each group got, not necessarily what it wanted, but what was best for it within the Marxist framework. Lenin never had any faith in the proletariat's ability to choose the right path without intellectual leadership. His system depended on a pyramid of power with one strong leader at its apex, and was benevolent only so long as that leader was benevolent.

But now the October Manifesto had soothed many, and winter was coming on. As the cold weather cooled the revolutionaries' ardor, the old authorities reestablished themselves, and the concessions of the October Manifesto were gradually revoked. On December 3 government troops invaded the Soviet and arrested all the members present.* The Moscow Soviet, which was largely Bolshevik, went down fighting. It called a

---

* About 300 were arrested and 52 were put on trial. Of these, 15, including Trotsky, received life sentences. On his way to Siberia, Trotsky escaped.

general strike which grew into warfare, with about 8,000 workers, armed with makeshift weapons, trying to hold out against
the tsar's dragoons. They lasted less than a week before suc-
cumbing to heavy artillery.

The revolutionary Soviet had lasted only 50 days, and now
it was time for Lenin to hide again. He had no place for heroics
in his scheme, and took every precaution against being isolated
or executed before he had completed his job. Now he holed up
in Finland, where he could be close to the revolutionaries in
Russia, but in less danger of arrest. (He made frequent trips
back into Russia.) Since Finland was then a Russian territory,
his freedom was far from guaranteed. In fact, the Okhrana
(secret police) knew where he was, but left him alone for
rightist reasons: they thought that without his disruptions, the
Mensheviks and Bolsheviks would reunite and become twice as
powerful.* They were probably right on the first count—the
two factions would have reunited—but wrong on the second.
The most prominent Mensheviks were types for whom the
moment of revolution would never have come. They were by
nature pacifistic and conciliatory on large issues, even though
they were never able to agree with each other.

In April, 1905, the Third Party Congress of Social Democrats had taken place in London without the Mensheviks, who
had held their own meeting in Geneva. The Fourth (Unity)
Congress found both factions under one roof in Stockholm, in
April, 1906, but their differences were more pronounced, if
anything. The Bolsheviks were in a minority now, but much
better united than the Mensheviks, who could agree on nothing.
Typically, the Mensheviks were generally pro-Duma and advo-

* Years later, from 1911 to 1914, Lenin was to place enormous trust
in Roman Malinovsky, who rose from Bolshevik ranks to membership
in the seven-man Bolshevik Central Committee. He was one of the six
Bolshevik deputies to the Fourth Duma. And not until 1914 did they
discover that he had, in fact, been an Okhrana agent all along. Lenin
had trusted Malinovsky because they seemed to think alike, but it would
seem that Malinovsky's dislike of the Mensheviks was an attempt to
keep the Social Democrats weak.

cated peaceful reforms, while arguing among themselves on how best to reform peaceably. The Bolsheviks were just as predictably anti-Duma, and were for armed uprising.

Lenin was against both the First Duma (convened in 1906) and the Second Duma (convened in 1907), because he thought they might accomplish enough to postpone the revolution. He supported later Dumas because by then it was too late for them to be effective.

In April, the month of the Social Democrats' Fourth Congress, the tsar at last met the demand for a Duma. But when its proposed reforms were outlined to him, he found them "inadvisable." The deputies argued among themselves and made speeches until July 9, when members arriving for a session at the Tauride Palace found the tsar's troops in possession, and were told that Nicholas had dissolved the Duma. The tsar was still Lenin's best ally.

But the uprising had left everyone sick of violence, and in 1906 there were signs of pacification everywhere in Russia. Lenin tried to think of the lost chance as a rehearsal for "his" revolution later on, and went on planning. He told his agitators to promise land to the peasants. Lenin realized the pitfalls in such a promise. He agreed with Marx that the village produced little except idiocy, and ideally would have assimilated the peasants into the proletariat as farm workers. But the peasants would have resisted that strenuously, and any workable government would have to have their support, at least at first. They wanted land, so he promised them land. It was a simple approach, and completely practical.

Lenin was now advocating "partisan activities," which is to say, crimes which would aid the cause, including the robbing of post offices and banks.* He had never advocated terrorism

---

* An outstanding raid in Tiflis in the summer of 1907 netted the revolutionaries 324,000 rubles. A young Bolshevik named Josef Dzhugashvili (Stalin) was one of the robbers. These crimes were to cause Lenin some embarrassment in later years, when he was the legal head of the state.

as an end in itself, and did not want terrorists in the party. They were too apt to be psychopaths or double agents, men who loved violence for its own sake and were loyal to no cause. But since the party needed money, and there were few revolutionaries who had it to give, the robberies had Lenin's approval.

Finally, he decided it was time to go abroad again. (He seems to have had a sort of sixth sense for police activity; shortly after his departure, arrests decimated the Bolshevik organization in Russia.) At the end of 1907, Lenin and Krupskaya left for Europe. During the next five and one-half years, they lived in Geneva, Paris, Stockholm, Berlin, and London. They had few possessions and moved as revolutionary activity dictated. For example, they went from Finland to Geneva, but April, 1908, found Lenin visiting the exiled Maxim Gorky in Capri, and May took him to London's British Museum, where he was gathering data for *Materialism and Empirio-Criticism*, a book which sought to show that philosophers who would contradict Marx were unsound. As usual, this was propaganda. Bolsheviks were wrangling over the philosophies of Ernst Mach and Richard Avenarius, and Lenin was afraid these quarrels would wreck the party.

Krupskaya wrote that these were "difficult times. In Russia the organizations were going to pieces. The police, with the aid of agents provocateurs, had arrested the leading party workers. . . . The masses withdrew into themselves . . . ; agitation . . . had palled and no longer satisfied anyone."* Depressed by the failure of the revolution and the plight of the party, Lenin said he felt as if he had returned to Geneva to "lie down in my grave." But he went on working; splinter groups emerged during these years—Recallers, Ultimatists, Liquidators—Lenin fought them all. In 1911 he organized a party school near Paris; he was now prepared to force a break with the Mensheviks and other subgroups, even if the Bolsheviks who remained

* Krupskaya, *Reminiscences of Lenin*, p. 183.

Photographs of Trotsky taken by the police in 1913.

with him were few. (He held a conference in Prague in January, 1912, and only 20 persons attended.)

By June, 1912, Lenin had decided to move closer to Russia; he went to Cracow, in Austria-Hungary. (Poland did not exist as a political entity in 1912.) He had chosen Cracow not only for its proximity to the Russian border, but because it was an area hostile to tsardom. His house became a meeting place for Russian revolutionaries during the next two years.

International troubles were obviously brewing. A full-scale war, added to Russia's already unsound economy, would be very good for the revolution. Lenin began preaching nationalism in an attempt to hasten the conflict. He knew that nationalism was, in Russia, a stronger force than any political system. It was even apparent in the revolutionaries. After the revolution, he was to say, "Scratch a Russian Communist and you will find a Russian chauvinist." Whether he knew it or not, he was one himself. He preached "international communism" and genuinely hoped for it, but he always thought in terms of Russian problems and solutions. He was extraordinarily good at predicting events in his own country, but not in others.

Then, in 1914, a Serbian terrorist assassinated the Austrian Archduke Franz Ferdinand, and gave Austria-Hungary an excuse to declare war on Serbia. Russia, traditionally the protector of all Slavs, automatically mobilized. Germany, equally enmeshed with Austria, demanded that the Russians stay out of it, and when the Russians refused, declared war on Russia on July 19, 1914 (August 1, New Style). France had a treaty with Russia and ties with England. . . . Suddenly world war erupted.

4. The End of the Autocracy

Lenin was technically an enemy alien in Cracow when the war began, but the Austrians, knowing he would do the tsarist government all the harm he could, held him less than two weeks before letting him leave for neutral Switzerland.

The next three years were very hard. Lenin had been a professional revolutionary since the age of 18; now he was in his mid-forties and his health was not good. Most of his adult life had been spent on the move. He had worked harder than most men at his profession, and had never expected it to make him rich, but now he was discouraged.* His ideas were disputed everywhere, and it looked as though he would lose the leadership of the Bolsheviks. He was particularly depressed by the patriotism of the world's socialists, and felt that the German Social Democrats had betrayed Marx by their whole-hearted support of the war. (It was now that he began calling

* Lenin's mother had always sent money, but her pension had died with her in the summer of 1916. Krupskaya's mother's legacy to them had been swallowed up in the costs of transferring money in wartime, and Lenin and Krupskaya were living from hand to mouth. In February 1917 Lenin wrote his sister Maria about having received money from Russia without any idea who had sent it or why. He said Krupskaya had joked about it and had told him he was beginning to draw a pension.

his party Communist, to find a label not "corrupted" by contact with such groups.)

The Russians had also been astonishingly eager to fight, considering the fiasco of the Russo-Japanese war, only nine years before. But again, inefficiency and dishonesty in both civil and military administration, added to chronically inadequate communications and transportation, soon brought demoralization. (During the general retreat of 1915, War Minister Polivanov said, "I place my trust in the impenetrable spaces, impassable mud, and the mercy of St. Nicholas Mirlikisky, Protector of Holy Russia." All three together were no substitute for modern weapons, training, and transportation.) Russia tried to make up in men what she lacked in equipment and technology— some soldiers were sent to the front unarmed—and casualties were very high. Between August, when the war began, and December, the Russians lost 300,000 men and 650 cannons. Desertions increased, and to reman the ranks, more and more peasants were conscripted and sent to the front with almost no training. The army's discipline began to go. Lost battles and an overburdened economy demoralized the civilian population too. Lenin, in Switzerland, might have reminded himself, "The worse it is, the better it is."

On January 22, 1917, he lectured young socialists in Zurich, ending sadly, "We of the older generation may not live to see the decisive battles of this coming revolution." This is often quoted as proof of Lenin's pessimism, but since he was speaking of international revolution, he was being realistic, if not optimistic. As late as May, 1917, he observed that "in other countries it will be more difficult [to accomplish a revolution]. There, there will not be half-witted people such as Nicholas and Rasputin. There the better people of their class are at the head of the government."*

* V. I. Lenin, *Lenin o Mezhdunarodnoi Politike i Mezhdunarodnom Prave* (Lenin on International Policy and International Law) (Moscow: Institute of International Relations, 1958), pp. 298–299.

In Russia, time was running out for Nicholas and Rasputin. As defeat followed defeat, the people looked for a scapegoat, and remembered that the tsarina had once been a German princess. They thought they saw evidence that the royal family was betraying Russia to the Germans. (There seems to have been no basis for this belief. If Nicholas gave aid and comfort to the enemy, it was the result of his ineptitude rather than of treachery.)

Nicholas was a sincere nationalist, but stupid, stubborn, and naive. He had learned nothing of value from the 1905 uprising, and Tsarina Alexandra encouraged his worst traits as a ruler. No peasant believed that the tsar was appointed by God more completely than she did. She felt that demonstrations and up- risings were an impertinence at the least, and that he should pay no attention to them unless it was to punish the offenders. He was greatly influenced by her. They were devoted parents, and concern for their only son, the heir Alexsei, had led to a stranger-than-fiction situation. Alexsei was a hemophiliac, and the slightest injury caused him to hemorrhage. The court physicians were powerless to help the boy, and when a self- styled "holy man," the Siberian peasant-monk Grigori Rasputin, proved to be able to stop the bleeding by staring at Alexsei, the royal couple opened all doors to him.

During his six years of influence, Rasputin used his powers of persuasion (some said he consciously hypnotized) to make himself virtually the uncrowned ruler. He was a lusty man, a hedonist of the sort whom the tsar and the tsarina would ordi- narily not have tolerated. (Trotsky called him "a crowned hooligan.") But the royal couple rejected reports of his licen- tiousness as lies of the jealous. They called Rasputin "Our Friend," told him everything, and took his advice on all mat- ters. He appointed and dismissed high officials as he chose, especially after Nicholas left for the front in September, 1915. Rasputin's behavior was a daily scandal. "His life in Petrograd became a continuous revel, the drunken debauch of a galley slave who had come into an unexpected fortune," said Prince Yusupov, who, with a small group of his peers, decided that Rasputin had been allowed to live too long. On December 16, 1916, they set about killing him. They served him little cakes containing potassium cyanide, which he ate without apparent ill effect. So they shot him. He revived, and they shot him again. At last they threw him into the freezing Neva River.

But if Rasputin was gone, so were the ablest men of the administration. The tsar was impatient in his stupidity, and disliked being corrected, contradicted, or reminded of unpleasantness. He had gradually weeded out all the most competent officials. The royal couple's attitude was the revolutionaries' trump card.

Nicholas's presence at the front could not help morale in the face of daily defeat. As battles were lost, the economy suffered in complex ways. Since the Third Partition of Poland in 1795, Russia had controlled a large part of that country. Coal mines and factories there were essential even to Russia's peacetime economy; now the Germans occupied that area. Russian production, inadequate in the best of times, was 50 percent converted to war materials. Civilian necessities were more and more scarce. The peasants had been conscripted by the thousands, and there weren't enough left on the land to plant and harvest. Transportation was going from bad to worse. There was hunger in the cities and profiteering everywhere. Petrograd's rich complained of the servant problem, but servants who earned about 35 rubles a month refused to stand in food lines and wear out the shoes that cost them 100 rubles. In Moscow, food prices increased on an average of 556 percent between August, 1914, and August, 1917. During the same period wages increased about 500 percent, but the price of necessities other than food rose an average of 1,109 percent. For example, men's shoes went from 12 rubles to 144 rubles, and a man's suit from 40 to 400 rubles. Living standards, which had never been high except for the rich, continued to deteriorate. The scene was set for a real revolution.

Soldiers demonstrating in Petrograd in April, 1917.

But when it came, it took everyone by surprise, even the socialists in Petrograd. It began with a strike, but there had been 575 strikes in January and February of 1917.* Everyone was used to strikes, and the revolution started with just one more: on February 23, International Women's Day, the female textile workers struck of their own accord. The men of the Putilov Works had been locked out, and they joined in the demonstration. That day, 50 factories were closed and 90,000 workers demonstrated, prompted mostly by hunger and fury. Most of the banners said simply, "BREAD!"

By the following day, there were 200,000 marchers out, and

* On the anniversary of Bloody Sunday, January 9, 150,000 workers had demonstrated.

now the slogans included "Down with the Autocracy." Again, the uprising was spontaneous and undirected, but now the revolution was close enough to cast a shadow: the Cossacks were there, but they made no move to interfere. They even let the people pass back and forth under their horses. On the 25th, there was a general strike. Newspapers stopped publishing and about 240,000 workers and their sympathizers crowded the streets. General Khabalov, chief of the Petrograd Military District, had just received a telegram from the tsar ordering him to suppress the disorders. The general, to enforce the order, informed all men registered for the draft that they would be sent to the front if they did not return to work by the 28th. He also ordered the police to fire on the demonstrators. But the revolution was on the doorstep; when the mounted police fired on the demonstrators, the Cossacks fired on the police! Incredible!

The police forces disintegrated, and were replaced by the army, but the common soldier needed little agitation to remind him that he was firing on his own people. On the 26th, soldiers were ordered to shoot into crowds in four different parts of Petrograd. Forty persons were killed and many more wounded. Since the Pavlovsky Regiment's training squad was among the firing soldiers, and had been equipped with machine guns, casualties might have been much higher. But the soldiers had no stomach for this sort of thing; that afternoon the men of the Pavlovsky agreed among themselves that they would not fire on a crowd again. The army mutinies had begun.* The Preobrazhensky, Litovsky, and Moscow regiments followed Pavlovsky.

Most of the police had gone into hiding when the tsar, from Supreme Army Headquarters in the Ukraine, ordered the Duma to stop meeting until April. The Duma received the edict

---

* The authorities were aware of the soldiers' feelings; the police report put the cause of the mutiny as "indignation against the training squad of the same regiment, which while on duty in the Nevsky, fired on the crowd."

on February 26, and the rioters heard of it on the 27th. Crowds immediately converged on the Tauride Palace, where the Duma sat, to show their support. Most Duma members were more upset by the crowd than by the edict. The conservative Shulgin wrote in his diary:

> The interminable, inexhaustible stream . . . threw itself into the Duma. . . . But no matter how many of them there were—they had one face: vile—animal—stupid . . . or wicked . . . God, how foul it was! So foul that I clenched my teeth, I felt within myself a sadness, powerlessness, and thus a still more malicious rage. . . . Machine guns! Machine guns—I wanted them. For I felt that only the language of machine guns would be understood by the street crowds and that only lead would be able to drive this terrible escaped beast back into his den. . . . Alas—this beast was . . . His Majesty the Russian people. . . . That which we so dreaded, that which we wanted to avoid was already a fact. The revolution had begun.*

On February 26, Mikhail Rodzianko, the president of the Duma, telegraphed Nicholas about the crisis. When no answer had come by the 27th, he sent an agonized appeal, saying that the government could not suppress the disorders, that the troops were in revolt, and that if the tsar did not take action at once, it might mean the end of the dynasty. "In the name of all Russia, I implore your Majesty to fulfill these suggestions. The hour which will decide your fate and that of the motherland has struck. Tomorrow may be already too late." The tsar said, "Again that fat-bellied Rodzianko has written me a lot of nonsense which I won't even bother to answer."

However, on February 28, Nicholas left the front for Tsarskoe Selo, where the tsarina and their children—who had the measles—were staying. By now even the tsarina was advising him to compromise, or at least to pretend to compromise, until

---

* Vasilii V. Shulgin, *Dni* (Days) (Leningrad, 1927), p. 136.

the revolutionaries could be crushed. Nicholas wired her: "Wonderful weather. Hope you are well and calm. Many troops sent from the front. With tender love, Niki." The tsar, always interested in the weather and his wife, was incapable of realizing the danger. But the revolutionaries held stations and bridges, and his train had to be diverted before it reached Tsarskoe Selo.

General Ivanov was more successful; he reached Tsarskoe Selo and telegraphed General Khabalov, chief of the Petrograd Military District, 10 questions:*

QUESTION: How many troops are in order and how many are misbehaving?
ANSWER: I have at my disposal in the Admiralty building four companies of the Guard, five squadrons of cavalry and Cossacks, and two batteries; the rest of the troops have gone over to the revolutionists, or by agreement with them are remaining neutral. Soldiers are wandering through the town singly or in bands disarming officers.

Q: Which railroad stations are guarded?
A: All the stations are in the hands of the revolutionists and strictly guarded by them.

Q: In what parts of the city is order preserved?
A: The whole city is in the hands of the revolutionists. The telephone is not working, there is no communication between different parts of the city.

Q: What authorities are governing the different parts of the city?
A: I cannot answer this question.

Q: Are all the ministries functioning properly?
A: The ministers have been arrested by the revolutionarists.

* Leon Trotsky, *The History of the Russian Revolution,* trans. Max Eastman, 3 vols. (Ann Arbor: University of Michigan Press, 1932), 1:84–85.

Q: What police forces are at your disposal at the present moment?
A: None whatever.

Q: What technical and supply institutions of the War Department are now in your control?
A: I have none.

Q: What quantity of provisions is at your disposal?
A: There are no provisions at my disposal. In the city on February 5 there were 5,600,000 poods of flour in store. [A pood equals 36 pounds.]

Q: Have many weapons, artillery and military stores fallen into the hands of the mutineers?
A: All the artillery establishments are in the hands of the revolutionists.

Q: What military forces and staffs are in your control?
A: The chief of the Staff of the District is in my personal control. With the other district administrations I have no connections.

Such information prompted the tsar's highest generals to plead that he abdicate in order to save the empire, and on March 2 he did, naming his son Alexsei successor and his brother, the Grand Duke Mikhail, as regent. Kadet leader Pavel Nikolaevich Miliukov noted, "The one is a sick child, the other an utterly stupid man."* Liberal monarchist V. N. Shidlovsky added his recommendation: "Mikhail Alexandrovich [the grand duke] has tried every way possible to avoid interfering in any affairs of state, devoting himself wholeheartedly to horseracing."† (Shidlovsky wanted Mikhail as a sort of ornament for a constitutional government.) But Mikhail was not utterly stupid after all, he declined the honor. It was too late to save the autocracy. On March 8 the tsar was placed

* *Ibid.,* p. 174.
† *Ibid.*

under house arrest, and in April, 1918, Nicholas, Alexandra, and their children were imprisoned in the Ural Mountains. On July 16, they were shot to death.

When the tsar was deposed, there was no longer any denying that this was a revolution. Petrograd found itself with two new governments; the Duma had disobeyed the tsar's order to dissolve, and instead had selected a committee to appoint a ministry. The result was the Provisional Government, which assumed office in the Tauride Palace on March 3. Its program included freedom of speech, press, and assembly and of striking and forming unions; amnesty for political and religious prisoners; the abolition of legal restrictions based on class, religion, or country of origin; the substitution of a people's militia for the old police force; and local administrations elected by secret ballot. As for the war, the Provisional Government wanted a victory, and intended to honor the tsar's treaties. The Allies therefore welcomed it—the United States was the first to do so, on March 9. The United States also loaned it $325,000,000 to try to strengthen the tottering economy.

The second government was the Soviet of Workers' and Soldiers' Deputies, risen again from the ashes of 1905. It purported to represent the masses, but in fact represented the deputies' individual views of what the masses ought to want. It was more like a socialist reunion than a legislature; its thousands of members included every type of Socialist Revolutionary and Social Democrat, as well as independents, all making endless speeches. Among its immediate goals were an eight-hour day, land redistribution, army reforms, and an early peace—by negotiation, not victory. It was an unwieldy, exasperating group, with internal dissensions that kept it from acting as a concerted force, but it had more real power than the Duma because the common people identified with it, and it could count on support from the vital services—postal workers, telegraph operators, railroad workers, and finally, the army.

The Soviet had promised army reforms, and certainly they

were long overdue. But Order No. 1, issued on March 1—before the tsar abdicated—was an invitation to anarchy. It commanded soldiers to ignore the old chain of command, and instead organize their own soviets, elect their own officers, and control all weapons. Later, the Soviet maintained that this directive had been meant only for the soldiers of Petrograd, but it swept the entire army. The old regimentation was thrown out, and no new order replaced it.

Contemplated land reforms also led to confusion; the rumor that the land was up for grabs was enough to make thousands of peasant conscripts desert. The Soviet had no immediate plans for land redistribution, the problems were too great, but it had good intentions, and kept saying so. The peasants stood on the land in full expectation of owning it. They were peaceable at first; there was no point in seizing land when it was still frozen. But with the planting season the countryside became a battleground. The well-meaning Soviet had pushed the country closer to civil war. This was not a Bolshevik conspiracy; the Bolsheviks in the Soviet were too few, and such leadership as they had on the scene was conciliatory. On March 12 three Bolsheviks recently returned from exile, Stalin, Leo Borisovich Kamenev, and M. Muranov, took over *Pravda*; on March 15 the paper announced the new editorship and its policy: it would support the Provisional Government "insofar as it struggles against reaction or counterrevolution." And if the German soldiers continued to fight, these Bolsheviks would support Russia's part in the war, advising Russian soldiers to "answer bullet with bullet and shell with shell" until the government could make a (hopefully) early peace. Many Bolshevik workers were furious, and those from the Vyborg district insisted that *Pravda* print their protest. "If the paper does not want to lose the confidence of the workers, it must and will bring the light of revolutionary consciousness, no matter how painful it may be, to the bourgeois owls."*

* Trotsky, *History of Russian Revolution,* 1:291.

Lenin was furious too. On March 12 he had written regarding the Provisional Government: "Our tactic: complete lack of confidence; no support of the new government; suspect [Alexander] Kerensky [its leader] especially; arming of the proletariat the sole guarantee; immediate elections to the Petrograd Duma; no rapprochement with other parties." The new editors' position was completely opposed to his. He fumed, helpless, in Geneva. The revolution had happened without him, he couldn't get home, and the Russian Bolsheviks were behaving like Mensheviks.

5. Lenin's Return to Russia

Krupskaya wrote of how news of the revolution had reached them in Geneva. It was

> after dinner, when Ilyich was getting ready to leave for the library, and I had finished with the dishes. Bronsky [a Polish revolutionary] ran in with the announcement. "Haven't you heard the news? There is a revolution in Russia!"*

Lenin and Krupskaya hurried "to the lake, where . . . all the newspapers were hung up as soon as they came out." Lenin was terribly excited, and "burned with eagerness" to direct the Bolsheviks in person. But how to get back? Those exiled socialists who advocated support of the Provisional Government and the continuing of the war would be sent home in style by the Allies, and welcomed in Russia. But the Russian consuls had been telegraphed to exclude Internationalists from expatriation plans. Even the Soviet could not be counted on. It had a very small Bolshevik membership, and its Mensheviks (its chairman, Nikolai Chkheidze, was a Menshevik) had all the internal dissension they needed without Lenin. Nevertheless, when Lenin's telegrams to Russia went unanswered, he got a Swedish

* Krupskaya, *Reminiscences of Lenin*, p. 199.

Marxist to send a personal emissary to Chkheidze. Since Chkheidze could hardly refuse to admit a fellow Social Democrat, he wired that Lenin should come home. He didn't say how.

Lenin tried all possible contacts, but nothing happened. The Swiss government ignored his requests. He gave his whole mind to the problem. Krupskaya wrote,

> Ilyich did not sleep, and at night all sorts of incredible plans were made. We could travel by airplane. But such things could be thought of only in the semi-delirium of the night. . . . A passport of a foreigner from a neutral country would have to be obtained, a Swedish passport would be best as a Swede arouses less suspicion . . . but there was the further obstacle of our not knowing the Swedish language . . . it would be so easy to give one's self away. "You will fall asleep and see Mensheviks in your dreams and you will start swearing, and shout, scoundrels, scoundrels! and give the whole conspiracy away," I said to him teasingly.*

Lenin thought of several rash schemes, but was no nearer Russia when, on March 19, there was a meeting of exiles to consider the problem. There, Martov† suggested that they might obtain permits enabling them to pass through Germany, in exchange for Russian-held German and Austrian prisoners of war. The other exiles were unenthusiastic, but Lenin "snatched at this plan." The others foresaw that such a method would leave them vulnerable to charges of conspiracy, of having spied for Germany. Lenin realized it too, but his desire to go was stronger than his caution. He did try to set up safe-

---

* *Ibid.,* p. 200.

† Julius Martov, born Tsederbaum, had been Lenin's close friend during their early revolutionary years, but had gone with the Mensheviks at the time of the split. This killed the friendship—for Lenin, there was no separating politics and personalities—but Lenin seems to have retained affection for his old friend, now an opponent. Martov was an Internationalist, which is why he too was stranded in Switzerland.

guards in advance, but his overriding concern was to get back. Krupskaya wrote that he would have made a deal with the devil in order to get home.

Waiting was a torment, but Lenin filled the hours by writing "Letters from Afar" for publication in *Pravda*. Like all his writing, they were in response to events, with titles like, "On Proletarian Militia" and "Problems of Revolutionary Proletarian Organization of the State." They made specific suggestions: the people's militia was to replace conventional police forces, and be used not only for traditional police purposes, but to distribute food (according to need, rather than by ability to pay), to help the homeless find shelter in the houses vacated by the nobility, and so forth. Many of the schemes he outlined were to be a part of his own administration, but others were simply rhetoric. He railed against the Provisional Government, with its bourgeois members and "imperialistic" outlook. He repudiated the tsarist government's debts and contracts, and advocated publication of secret treaties, immediate withdrawal from the war, and the liberation of all dependencies. The fifth letter remained unfinished; Lenin was going home.

Krupskaya wrote that when Lenin received word that the negotiations were complete, he would tolerate no further delay. He said,

> "We will take the first train." The train was due to leave within two hours. We had just those two hours to liquidate our entire "household," settle accounts with the landlady, return the books to the library, pack up and so on. "Go yourself, I will leave tomorrow, I said. But Ilyich insisted, "No, we will go together." In the two hours everything was done.*

Fritz Platten, the Swiss Socialist-Internationalist, had concluded a written agreement with the German ambassador. In effect, it guaranteed extraterritoriality to the travelers. The

* *Ibid.,* p. 208.

main points of it, according to Krupskaya, were that all emigrants, regardless of their stand on the war, would be allowed
to go; that no one would be allowed to enter their railway car
without Platten's permission; that there would be no inspection
of passports or baggage; and that, in return, the travelers
promised to try to agitate for the exchange of Austrian and
German prisoners equal to the number of emigrants who returned to Russia.*

Many Western writers later told the world that Lenin had
traveled in a "sealed train"; in fact, the train was sealed by
nothing more than the revolutionaries' determination not to
leave themselves open to charges of collaboration with the
enemy. Many accounts also said that when Lenin entered his
compartment, he found there a man suspected of being a German spy, and promptly and wordlessly threw the man out.
Krupskaya and Lenin do not mention such an incident, and in
view of the fact that Lenin was only five feet, six inches tall,
and never inclined to personal violence, it seems unlikely.
Krupskaya wrote of the trip:

> The comrades going to Russia met in the Berne People's
> House. . . . Altogether, thirty people . . . [not counting a four-
> year-old].
> . . . Of course, in giving us permission to travel, the German
> government was under the impression that revolution was a
> terrible disaster for a country and thought . . . they would help
> to spread this "disaster" in Russia. The Bolsheviks were very
> little concerned with what the bourgeois German government
> thought. They considered it their duty to spread revolutionary

---

* The question of why the Germans were willing to go to all this
trouble in return for the problematical return of ordinary prisoners of
war lies in the character of the Internationalists, especially Lenin. The
Germans undoubtedly tried to hire him to work for them, but in any
case, they believed that his disruptive qualities would serve their cause
in Russia. Lenin had been preaching fraternization with the enemy and
an immediate end to the war.

propaganda in Russia and set as the aim of their activities the achievement of the victorious proletarian revolution. . . .

In boarding the train, no questions were asked about the baggage and passports. Ilyich kept entirely to himself, his thoughts were in Russia. . . .

. . . Near Berlin several German Social-Democrats entered a special compartment. No one of our people spoke to them, except . . . [the four-year-old] . . . they were not able to put the questions they wanted to . . . to the Bolsheviks.*

On March 31 they arrived in Sweden, where the Swedish Marxists had prepared a welcome, with food and banners. They took Lenin shopping; he let himself be talked into buying new shoes, but balked at an overcoat, saying that he was not returning to Russia to open a tailor's shop. Soon they were ready to resume their trip. Krupskaya remembered, "From Sweden we crossed to Finland in small Finnish sledges. Everything was already familiar and dear to us—the wretched third-class cars, the Russian soldiers. It was terribly good."

The travelers were nearing the border. Lenin had wired that he and Krupskaya were coming, and his sister Maria was among the Bolsheviks who boarded the train at Beloostrov, to ride the last part of the journey with their leader. Kamenev came too. "What's this you're writing in *Pravda?*" Lenin asked him. The two were nevertheless glad to see each other. In such a situation, Lenin's method was never to back an opponent into a corner, but always to leave room for him to change his stand without "losing face." The train was running very late, but at 11:10 on the night of April 3, it pulled into Petrograd's Finland Station.

The travelers stepped onto Russian soil and into a most extraordinary scene. The platform was lined with soldiers presenting arms. Banners and triumphal arches gleamed red and gold. The band played the "Marseillaise" and representatives of

* *Ibid.,* pp. 208–209.

the Bolshevik Central Committee carried bouquets. (It is still a Russian custom to welcome heroes with flowers.) This had been a week of gala greetings, of exiles returning, and the Bolsheviks were not to be outdone. An honor guard of people's militia and of sailors from the naval base at Kronstadt lined the entrance through which Lenin would pass to what had formerly been the tsar's waiting room. Krupskaya was speechless at "the sea of people."

The Menshevik Sukhanov* saw the whole thing, and recorded it. He said that Lenin came in on the run, looking chilled and carrying a magnificent bouquet. When he neared Chkheidze, he stopped short, "as though colliding with a completely unexpected obstacle." Considering what he had called the Menshevik leader, often in print, Lenin could hardly have anticipated that he would head the welcoming committee. Chkheidze had not wanted to come, but it was only proper that the Soviet be represented—socialists have their etiquette too—so he and Matvei Ivanovich Skobelev, the Menshevik minister of labor, were there. They had been waiting for hours, and Chkheidze had become more and more morose. Now he had to swallow his Menshevik misgivings and behave like a socialist comrade, but his welcome had, according to Sukhanov, "not only the spirit and wording, but also the tone of a sermon." He said,

Comrade Lenin, on behalf of the Petrograd Soviet of Workers' and Soldiers' Deputies and all the revolution, we welcome you to Russia. But—we believe that the chief task of revolutionary democracy just now is the defense of our revolution from every

* Sukhanov was born Nikolai Nikolayevich Himmer, but his revolutionary name was N. N. Sukhanov, and that is how he signed as author of a seven-volume account of the 1917 revolution, a diarylike recollection of the days from February 21 through October 26. He was a Menshevik, and while, as an Internationalist, he had some sympathies with the Bolsheviks, his beliefs differed enough so that he and Lenin were highly critical of each other. Sukhanov wanted the SDs to unify, for example, which makes his view of events particularly interesting.

An artist's conception of Lenin's arrival at Finland Station. M. Sokolov painted this during Stalin's dictatorship and tactfully put Stalin on the train behind Lenin. Not only did Soviet artists add Stalin to group pictures, but they also removed former leaders who had fallen from Communist grace, such as Trotsky.

infringement upon it, from within and without. We believe that for this objective a rallying of all democratic ranks is necessary, not disunity. We hope that you will pursue these objectives together with us.*

Join the Mensheviks?! Lenin ignored both speech and speaker. He glanced around the room, "even examined the ceiling... while rearranging his bouquet." When Chkheidze finished, Lenin turned to the crowd and said,

Dear comrades, soldiers, sailors, and workers! I am happy to

* N. N. Sukhanov, *Zapiski o Revoliutsii* (Notes on the Revolution), 7 vols. (Berlin: Z. J. Grschebin, 1922), 2:14.

greet in you the victorious Russian Revolution, and welcome
you as the advanced detachment of the universal proletarian
army. The predatory imperialist war is the beginning of civil
war in all of Europe. The hour is not far off when . . . the
people will turn their weapons against their . . . exploiters. . . .
The Russian Revolution, absolutely due to you, is the beginning
and the inauguration of a new epoch. Long live the international
socialist revolution!*

This was something brand new to the assembled crowd. Sukhanov wrote of their reaction, as "absolutely absorbed by the
humdrum drudgery of the revolution . . . we were presented
with a blazing, dazzling, exotic beacon. Lenin's voice, ringing
out straight from the train, was a 'voice from the outside!' . . .
there burst upon us a truth . . . a note not discordant but novel,
harsh, somewhat stunning."†

So far, Lenin had been heard only by the dignitaries within
the room. Outside, a mob was trying to break down the glass
doors. The rank-and-file Bolsheviks were furious at having
been shut out while "complete strangers" were inside with
Lenin. Crowds blocked the whole square, red banners flew, and
a mounted searchlight illuminated the pandemonium. There
were not only passenger cars—scarce in Russia in those days—
but a whole armored car division, symbols of power. Lenin
went out, and they boosted him onto the hood of a car to make
another speech. The theme of all his public statements that
night was the same: end the "imperialistic" war through international revolution. Don't trust the Provisional Government,
"They are deceiving you and the whole Russian people. The
people need peace, the people need bread, the people need
land. And they give you war, hunger, and . . . leave the landlords still on the land."

The Bolsheviks had "liberated" Kshesinskaya's Palace for

* *Ibid.*, 2:15.
† *Ibid.*, 2:16.

their headquarters. (She was a ballerina, and a favorite of the tsar's. Her furniture had been removed, but the painted decorations and mirrors made an incongruous background for the revolutionaries.) Tonight they had planned a tea there to welcome Lenin. He traveled on an armored car, with a mounted searchlight, and made speeches at each cross-street. The band, workers' detachments, and army units were joined by crowds of socialists and curious members of the public.

The speeches were not what the crowd had expected, and such reaction as was voiced was hostile. The soldiers had been "organized" into coming as units by Bolshevik agitators. Many hardly knew who Lenin was. (Back at Finland Station, a young naval commander had, in the name of the sailors present, expressed the hope that Lenin would join the Provisional Government!). Now, some soldiers were heard to mutter that they'd like to teach Lenin a lesson with bayonets.

Sukhanov was allowed to follow the Bolsheviks into Kshesinskaya's Palace. He wrote that as he looked and listened to them, it seemed clear that "the best among them felt themselves to be dedicated servants, as knights were of the Holy Grail." The rank and file of the party, always to the left of the general leadership, hung on Lenin's every word, even if the message shocked more powerful men.

The evening had been planned as a social occasion, "a comradely tea" with welcoming speeches. But Lenin was impatient to get on with his revolution. Trotsky, who wasn't there but knew Lenin's habits very well, said that during the civilities he behaved like a pedestrian waiting in a doorway for the rain to stop. When he finally took the floor, he spoke for two hours, and what he said shook the room.

Lenin's speech was never officially recorded,* but it made

* Throughout this time, the Bolsheviks had no stenographers, and all speeches not published by their authors depended on journalists or other interested recorders for preservation, which is why many of them exist in various forms today.

such an impression that several who heard it wrote their recollections of it. Lenin said that civil war was inevitable. He dismissed the Soviet's peace policy and its proposed agrarian reforms, advocating that the peasants simply seize the land and hold it in peasant-elected committees. Similarly, he urged that workers be encouraged to take over their factories. As for the Provisional Government, he said, "We don't need a parliamentary republic, we don't need bourgeois democracy, we don't need any government except the Soviet of Workers', Soldiers', and Farm-Workers' Deputies." Lenin also told the Bolsheviks who'd advocated conciliation what he thought of them. He didn't name names—he was going to let them change their minds without calling attention to them, if they would. Sukhanov wrote that while Lenin did not use polished or elegant oratorical techniques, he was nevertheless "an orator of tremendous impact and power, breaking down complicated systems into the simplest and most generally understandable elements, and hammering, hammering, hammering them into the heads of his audience until he captured them."

Sukhanov also said that he left feeling as though he'd been "flogged over the head with a flail." He felt that he could never agree with Lenin, which is hardly surprising, since Sukhanov was never a Bolshevik. But many Bolsheviks were equally stunned. In trying to follow Lenin's arguments, they came up against first one blank wall and then another. In the first place, the soviets had not been thought of as governing bodies. They had grown out of strike committees, and reacted to, rather than made, events. Then, there was no formal linkage of separate soviets, each existed independently. To the listeners, it seemed that Lenin was advocating local authority without any central government. Up until this time, even the Bolsheviks had envisioned a new state which somehow incorporated the old order.

They had also been moving toward unity with other socialists. Stalin had written, of reunion with the Mensheviks, "We must do it.... There is no party life without disagreements. We will live down our petty disagreements within the party."* These "petty disagreements" were what Krupskaya thought would give Lenin nightmares on the airplane.

Moreover, one of the rules that gave the Bolsheviks greater strength than larger parties was the insistence on public unanimity. They could argue among themselves for a time, but would then have to decide whether to endorse or repudiate Lenin's stand, as a party. Their initial reaction was baffled amazement; many predicted that he had commited political suicide.

It was dawn before Lenin and Krupskaya went home to Lenin's sister Anna's house. Maria was there as well as Anna, her husband, and their adopted son. Lenin was a family man— during the next few days he made time to decorate his mother's and sister's graves—but there was little time for reunion with the living. He had hardly had a nap when a comrade came to take him to the Soviet to report on the trip through Germany.

From the Soviet, Lenin went to the All-Russian Bolshevik Conference at the Tauride Palace. Here he presented the ideas since known as the April Theses. They outlined his appraisal of the revolution and his aims: he was against continuation of the war, and therefore for propaganda and agitation that would encourage fraternization with the enemy. He was against support of the Provisional Government, "a government of capitalists," and recognized only the Soviet, "the sole possible form of revolutionary government." He therefore thought that to go from a Soviet to a parliamentary republic would be "a step backward." He particularized: he wanted police, army, and bureaucracy replaced by a people's militia; he wanted all public officials elected, and subject to removal from office, and not paid more than "a good worker." He wanted to encourage

* Trotsky, *History of the Russian Revolution,* 1:305.

class-consciousness in the proletariat. He wanted to confiscate all landlords' land and to nationalize land generally, creating model farms. He wanted to nationalize the banks and put them under Soviet control. As for party problems, he wanted an immediate party congress to change the program of "imperialism and the imperialistic war," and several other domestic issues. He wanted the party's name officially changed from Social Democratic to Communist. And he wanted to revive the international conferences of socialists.

He was impatient with rhetoric, circumlocutions, and vacillation, and asked outright, "Why didn't you seize the power?" Comrade Yuri Steklov had rashly tried to explain that the revolution was bourgeois, in the first stage, and what with the war . . . Lenin said, "That's nonsense!" and voiced the belief that would guide his activity for months to come:

> The reason is that the proletariat was not sufficiently conscious and not sufficiently organized. The material force was in the hands of the proletariat but the bourgeoisie was conscious and ready. That is the monstrous fact. But it is necessary to acknowledge it frankly, and say to the people straight out that we did not seize power because we were unorganized and not conscious.*

To those who had been thinking in terms of achieving a democracy through cooperation with the Provisional Government, by means of a Constituent Assembly, Lenin said, ". . . life and the revolution will push the Constituent Assembly into the background. A dictatorship of the proletariat exists, but nobody knows what to do with it." Trotsky says that his words "passed over the work of the conference like the wet sponge of a teacher erasing what had been written on the blackboard by a confused pupil."

---

* *Ibid.*

But Lenin's followers had reason to be confused. His endorsement of the Soviet was a recent development; in 1905 he had paid it little attention. (It was a Menshevik invention.) But in the intervening years, he had realized that it was a ready-made bridge to the proletariat. He needed that bridge, and never hesitated to adopt his opponents' ideas if they would further his cause. But what about "All power to the Soviet"? The Soviet would have all power only if the Provisional Government ceased to exist. Suppose the government did fall, who would rule Russia? Certainly not the Petrograd Soviet, with its thousands of disagreeing members. It couldn't even govern itself. And if by some miracle the Petrograd Soviet pulled itself together and began to function as a legislature, could it legislate for Moscow, which had its own completely independent Soviet? What about the rest of the enormous country? Anarchy would result.

So far, Lenin and his followers—and his enemies—saw the problem similarly. The difference was that at this point others felt that they had encountered an insurmountable obstacle. But Lenin had selected a strong determined leader who he felt sure could use this anarchy to establish a socialist state—himself. No other group contested him because no other group wanted the responsibility for the impossible task of restoring and maintaining order. Even the other Bolsheviks whispered that "Ilyich had stayed too long abroad."

From the Bolshevik conference, Lenin went to a general meeting of Social Democrats, including Mensheviks and Independents. The conference had been called before Lenin's return for the express purpose of unifying all factions into a single party. There had been high hopes of unity; men of good will almost instinctively looked for bases for agreement. Moreover, many of these good Marxists were disposed to make this a bourgeois revolution not because they felt any affection for the class, but because Marx had said that capitalism must precede socialism. (The Provisional Government was a monument to Marx; it had no popular support, but the Soviet wanted it in power, criticizing it constantly, because this was the evolution outlined by Marx.) But Lenin had arrived, and Sukhanov, one of the leaders of the conciliation movement, called him "the living incarnation of schism." Lenin spoke for two hours, and his speech doomed the causes of unification and pacification completely.

Not that he received unanimous support; it was apparent that even the Bolsheviks were baffled. And the Mensheviks and Independents were incredulous. Stankevich, a Trudovik, said that "Lenin's speech greatly delighted his enemies. 'A man who talks that kind of stupidity is not dangerous. It's a good thing he has come. Now he is in plain sight. . . . Now he will refute himself.' "* Goldenberg (Meshkovsky) who had been a Bolshevik and would later rejoin the party, saw Lenin's theories as "primitive anarchism," and said that Lenin had "raised the banner of civil war within the democracy." Steklov, whom Sukhanov called "the future bard and 'ideologist' of Leninist policy," wrote a newspaper article calling Lenin's speech "abstract constructions demonstrating that the Russian Revolution has passed him by."† He added, "After Lenin gets acquainted with things in Russia, he will reject all these constructions." That was one general prediction; Sukhanov also believed that after Lenin had had a chance to see the difference between revolutionary theories and real revolution, he would become "practical" and forget his "anarchistic ravings," and that the pressure of other Bolsheviks would hasten the process.

Miliukov agreed. These were the men who thought that Lenin still had a future if he changed direction. There were others who thought that nothing could save him now, that he was, as Skobelev said, "a lost man standing outside the movement."

---

* *Ibid.,* 1:309.
† Sukhanov, *Zapiski o Revoliutsii,* 2:41.

Socialist Revolutionary Vladimir Mikhailovich Zenzinov recalled, "His program at that time was met not so much with
indignation as with ridicule. It seemed to everybody so absurd
and fantastic."*

On April 7 the Theses were printed in *Pravda* under Lenin's
name alone. At a time when dozens of names usually endorsed
any party publication, no Bolshevik organization or individual
had joined him. Moreover, *Pravda*'s editors printed their reaction, saying that the Theses were, in effect, the private opinion
of an eccentric, and were not endorsed by *Pravda* or the Bureau
of the Bolshevik Central Committee. Zalezhski, a member of
the Bolshevik Central Committee and one of the organizers of
Lenin's welcome, said, "Lenin's Theses produced the impression of an exploding bomb," adding that on April 4 "Comrade
Lenin could not find open sympathizers even in our own
ranks."†

Lenin's friends tried to get him to change his stand, to save
his career. But Lenin was not a mere politician, he had read
Pravda, knew that his stand was in direct contradiction to what
the Bolshevik leadership had been saying, and that he would
stand alone (he may not have realized how much alone). He
would battle for party leadership not out of personal ambition,
but because the party was the instrument he intended to use to
socialize Russia. Its present direction would, if continued, kill
chances for successful revolution, and he would rather have
gone down fighting than have compromised on these issues.

And while Lenin was having trouble with his friends, his
enemies attacked in force. He became the prime target in a
campaign against Bolshevism generally. The middle class demanded, "Down with Lenin—Back to Germany," and soldiers
and workers took up the cry. On April 14–16, the Baltic Fleet
crew which had distinguished itself in the revolution, and had

* Trotsky, *History of the Russian Revolution,* 1:310–311.
† *Ibid.,* 1:312.

formed the guard of honor for Lenin at Finland Station, published their feelings in all the Petrograd papers:

> Having learnt that Comrade Lenin returned to us in Russia with the assent of his Majesty the Emperor of Germany and King of Prussia . . . we express our profound regret at having participated in his festive welcome upon riding into Petrograd. If we had known by what ways he had returned to us, then in place of enthusiastic shouts of "Hurrah" our indignant cries would have resounded: "Back to the country across which you came to us!"*

Crowds assembled at Kshesinskaya's Palace to demonstrate against Lenin, and a mob marched, demanding that he be arrested. Sukhanov says that "Arrest Lenin," and "Down with the Bolsheviks" was heard at every street corner.

Lenin petitioned the Executive Committee of the Soviet to refute the slanders. The committee, which was largely Menshevik, exonerated him, noting that the whole thing was the Provisional Government's fault for not having helped him, and all other Internationalists, come home by less exotic means. Its paper, *Izvestia*, published a defense and counterclaims. Possibly the committee was generous because it felt that after his preposterous Theses, Lenin was no longer a threat.

It is interesting that all refutations of the charges insist that Lenin had not taken money from the Germans. But whether or not he had—and he probably had—is irrelevant. Lenin would have taken money from anyone, with no more feeling of obligation than he felt to the banks that the Bolsheviks had robbed. Any subversive activities of his were, and would be, to further the revolution. If they incidentally aided a foreign power, that was coincidence. He was impatient with socialists who spoke of honoring contracts and playing by the rules. He thought rules were for children's games. Trotsky agreed. Concerning aid to

---

* Sukhanov, *Zapiski o Revoliutsii,* 3:109.

the Germans, he said, "A suspicion against us in that direction could be expressed only by those who do not know what a revolutionary is."

Lenin had no time to brood, he was out meeting the workers. As usual, the rank-and-file Bolsheviks were far to the left of the leadership, and Lenin found support among them. In April, 1917, there were only about 79,000 Bolsheviks in all Russia, but about 15,000 of them were in Petrograd. He worked tirelessly among them; he had told the leaders, "Have done with greetings and resolutions! It's time to get down to business. We must proceed to practical sober work!"

For the next week, Lenin was everywhere, and at his most persuasive. He was fighting not only for his political life, but for the revolution. And when a general city conference of Petrograd Bolsheviks was held from April 14 to April 22, Lenin's views were accepted. The Central Committee's resolution of April 21–22 was virtually a summation of the Theses. On April 24, at the All-Russian Bolshevik Conference 140 delegates voted almost unanimously on resolutions embodying the Theses. It made them the official national platform and Lenin the undisputed leader of the Bolsheviks.

From outcast to leader; it was a remarkable about-face. Krupskaya attributed the party's change of heart partly to world events—in effect, to the rash acts of Lenin's enemies. On the seventh, the Executive Committee of the Petrograd Soviet had voted for the issue of a "liberty loan"—a war loan— which was against all Bolshevik principles. Then, the campaign against Lenin backfired. It popularized his Theses, and the common people liked what they heard. Non-Bolsheviks, such as soldiers, began showing interest, and Lenin spoke to them himself whenever he could. He made converts by the hundreds. The common people reasoned that the Theses were what they themselves believed; why should the leaders be making such a fuss about them? Had they in fact sold out to the middle class? Was this guilty consciences speaking? On April 10 Lenin ad-

dressed the Izmailovsky Regiment, and on the 16th the Petrograd soldiers and sailors organized a protest *against* the anti-
Lenin campaign.

Then there was the episode of Miliukov's Note to the Allies,
on April 18. Miliukov was the Provisional Government's foreign
minister. His note promised Britain and France that Russia
would continue the war, and would honor all existing treaties.
He anticipated criticism, because both the Provisional Government and the Soviet were supposed to have renounced the
treaties as containing clauses that no socialist could condone,
such as the annexation of Constantinople. But the Provisional
Government needed money, and to get it from the Allies, he
had to give them some such assurance. Moreover, he misjudged
his support. Shortly before he sent the note, thousands of
middle-class demonstrators had paraded on Nevsky Prospect—
Petrograd's main street—and on April 17 a huge crowd of
disabled veterans had come to Petrograd to demand war till
victory, and that Lenin be arrested and exiled. Miliukov had
overestimated the number of people represented by these two
groups, and thought that he could count on a majority of
Russians. Instead, he got the April Days.

When Miliukov's note fell into the Soviet's hands, on April
19, they published it in the Petrograd newspapers (April 20)
and demanded an explanation. Socialists at all levels thought
that the note negated the revolution. Factories emptied as
workers met and demonstrated. It was a spontaneous protest
similar to those that the workers had always staged, except that
this was not for food or pay, this was ideological. The agitators
must have felt triumphant; it had taken centuries to get the
workers to this point, and the soldiers were there too. When
25,000 workers marched on the Marian Palace with signs reading "Down with Miliukov," "Down with the Provisional Government," "Down with Guchkov" (Alexander Guchkov, the
war minister), the Finland Regiment marched with them.
Soldiers surrounded the palace and occupied all entrances and

exits. The Moscow and 180th regiments joined the Finland. The soldiers became ambitious; they decided to arrest not only Miliukov but the entire Provisional Government. The Provisional Government was alarmed for obvious reasons. The Soviet's alarm was more complicated, but just as real. Its members feared that if the Provisional Government fell, the Soviet would be forced to assume more responsibility than it wanted. Its delegates did not want to rule Russia.

Meanwhile, news of the note reached Moscow, and similar demonstrations took place. In both cities there was also reaction—supporters of Miliukov and the Provisional Government came out against the leftists. Shooting began and a civil war seemed imminent. The Provisional Government was powerless, but the Soviet acted: it forbade any street meetings or demonstrations for three days, through April 23. Its order was obeyed, and the civil war evaporated. The demonstrators' demands were met—Miliukov, Guchkov, and several other unpopular ministers were removed from office, and, the members of the Soviet's Executive Committee were invited to join the cabinet. The vote, taken on May 1, was 41 for coalition, 18 against, and 3 abstaining. The socialists accepted 6 of the 15 portfolios. The new cabinet repudiated the note, and Petrograd settled back into relative calm.

Certainly none of these events hurt Lenin, but Sukhanov, who never approved of the Theses or of the government they implied, gives the credit for their acceptance to Lenin himself. He calls Lenin "an extraordinary phenomenon . . . an unusually happy combination of theoretician and popular leader . . . a genius." His assessment of Lenin is one which others who knew him have voiced:

A genius is an abnormal man. . . . To be specific, this type of man quite often has an extremely limited sphere of intellectual activity, in which work is carried on with extraordinary strength and productivity. Quite often men of genius are extremely narrow

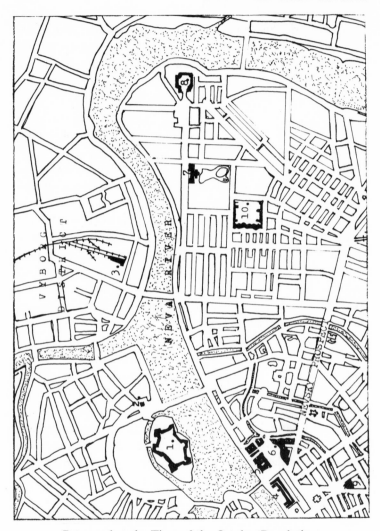

Petrograd at the Time of the October Revolution

1. Peter-Paul Fortress   6. Palace Square
2. Kshesinskaya's Palace   7. Tauride Palace
3. Finland Station   8. Smolny
4. Admiralty Building   9. Marian Palace
5. Winter Palace   10. Preobrazhensky Barracks

chauvinists to the core, have no understanding of, are not receptive to, are incapable of making sense of, the very simplest . . . things. Undoubtedly Lenin was like this also. Many elementary truths, even in the field of social movements, were inaccessible to Lenin's mind. But within a certain sphere of ideas—a few "fixed ideas"—Lenin manifested such amazing force, such superhuman power of attack that his colossal influence within the realm of socialists and revolutionaries was secure.

The genius Lenin was an historic authority. This is one side of the business. The other is that in the party, except for Lenin, there was no one and nothing. A few big generals—without Lenin nothing, like a few immense planets without the sun.*

Sukhanov also said that the April Days completed Lenin's education, and Lenin himself said that they showed him "the true meaning and role of a popular uprising."

* *Ibid.*, 2:52–55.

6. Building Bolshevik Might

Lenin won undisputed leadership of the Bolsheviks at a time when they were weaker than most other parties, and at a time when no party in Russia considered itself strong enough to rule the country. For the rest of 1917, Russia was virtually without a government; members of the Provisional Government and the Soviet made speeches while the country's economy slowed almost to a standstill.

The February Revolution is often referred to as bloodless. By Russian standards few persons were killed, and except for a mutiny at Kronstadt naval base, Petrograd alone had had casualities. (In Petrograd, the City Council estimated 1,315 dead—53 officers, 602 soldiers, 73 policemen, and 587 others.) But even in Petrograd, the violence had been unpremeditated, the result of spontaneous clashes of opposing forces on the spot. During the earliest days, there was almost none of the lawlessness associated with mob activity, such as looting, burning, or lynching, even though the jails were emptied of felons at the same time that the political prisoners were freed. Outside of the two capitals, Petrograd and Moscow, there was hardly any sign that the revolution had taken place. But when no new government replaced tsardom, conditions in the cities moved closer

"Bolshevik," a painting by B. Kustodiev.

and closer to anarchy, and instead of quieting, became more violent.

There was a saying that the women in the queues had made the revolution, and Sukhanov kept in touch with their attitudes through the old nurse of a colleague. He asked her whether the revolution had improved conditions; she said, "The queues aren't smaller, but are bound to become bigger. . . . You stand there half the day, just as before. . . . to us it makes no difference, the rich fleece the poor, only the shopkeepers are becoming rich."*

The Provisional Government was powerless to act, it had no

* *Ibid.,* pp. 64–65.

enforcement body and lacked popular support. The Soviet could not reach agreement among its members. No one was making any practical physical changes in the conditions which the people had protested for so long, and until they did, the uprisings would continue. The April Days proved it.

The April Days had also illuminated two new trends which encouraged the Bolsheviks. The first, which can hardly be overestimated, was the cooperation of soldiers and workers. This was something new; the autocracy had always used the army to repress demonstrations. In fact, the bourgeoisie had had hopes of reestablishing this tradition, and Sukhanov wrote that as late as March, 1917, the whole middle class was systematically trying to cause trouble between workers and soldiers. They sent agitators to the barracks with good results; during the last 10 days of March, "at every street crossing, in trams, or in any public place, you could see workers and soldiers . . . in furious verbal battle. There was also actual fighting."

The middle class tried to use the workers' demand for an eight-hour day to reestablish the old hostility between soldier and worker. Most of the soldiers were conscripted peasants, and the bourgeoisie reminded them that neither peasant nor soldier could hope for any such workday, adding that the laziness of the workers had resulted in shortages at the front. The soldiers at first were convinced by these arguments and threatened to invade the factories and force the workers to produce. But the scheme backfired. The Soviet worked hard to explain each group to the other, and the Petrograd proletariat—a group courted and bombarded by politicians from infancy, and perfectly able to recognize agitation—bent over backward to reassure the soldiers. It sent its own agitators, many of them Bolsheviks, to the army. It invited army representatives to the factories. It used all the techniques of persuasion, and in this case, it had the facts on its side. No one actually in the factories could fail to understand that it was lack of raw materials, not lazy workers, that was responsible for poor production. The army was won over to the proletariat's cause, and the Provisional Government's last hope of being able to call on military backing disappeared. The Soviet, long representative of the workers, now represented the soldiers as well. A French representative, M. Cachin, who toured Russia and returned home to report, explained why "gangs of workers and soldiers sitting in the Tauride Palace under the name of a Soviet . . . had not yet been dispersed. He said, 'Gentlemen, ten million bayonets are entirely at the disposal of the Soviet.' "

This was the second important illumination of the April Days—the power of the Soviet. From now on, any government that even wanted to pretend to function would have to include socialists. In May, the Kronstadt sailors announced that they would recognize no government except the Petrograd Soviet, but finally agreed to less drastic demands. Everyone was relieved; the Provisional Government enjoyed going through the motions of governing, the Soviet did not want to be handed sole governmental power, and Lenin did not really want the Soviet to have "all power" until he could make it a Bolshevik Soviet.

Moreover, now that Soviet delegates would also be ministers of the Provisional Government, they could be held responsible for unpopular policies.* Lenin took immediate advantage of this opening. He cried, "Down with the ten capitalist ministers" and spelled out his meaning: by entering the bourgeois government, the socialists had betrayed socialism and the revolution. He predicted darkly that the Provisional Government, if allowed, would lose no time in reestablishing the very power structure that the people had worked to overthrow.

The Provisional Government's policy toward the war illustrated his contention. The fighting had virtually stopped in February; now Kerensky, the popular Trudovik minister of war and of the admiralty, went to the front to try to rally the

---

* They were ministers of justice, supply, labor, and posts and telegraphs.

troops. He was planning a resumption of the fighting, and on May 14 ordered the army to go where its leaders commanded, adding that the soldiers would be carrying peace on their bayonet points and would be kept resolute by discipline and love for the revolution. The Provisional Government, for all its socialist representatives, still saw no way out of the war except through victory. (Socialist ideals were expressed in the rider, "without annexations or indemnities.") Victory relied on a successful offensive.

The decision was madness, the work of men too used to considering abstractions to give attention to such physical facts as lack of weapons, ammunition, and food. Kerensky reminded the troops that this time they would be fighting for themselves and the new Russia, not for the tsar. He was a persuasive orator, and a surprising number of soldiers were again ready to fight. On June 16 the new offensive began. Events might have turned out quite differently for the Bolsheviks if the soldiers had had any hope of winning, but victory was physically impossible. And it required no agitation to fix in the survivors' minds the connection between Kerensky, the Coalition Government, and the disastrous and demoralizing defeat.

The demoralization was felt by civilians too, and accentuated the polarization of the classes. All through the summer, the proletariat moved further and further to the left, and the upper classes further and further right. Petrograd's soldiers had remained prowar longer than had the men in Moscow or the provinces, but by May they were demonstrating against the war. At the end of the month, soldiers aged 40 or more marched through Petrograd in a column nearly two-thirds of a mile long; "its beginning and end were lost in the distance." They trudged in ominous silence, carrying signs which said, "Our Land Isn't Sown," "We Can't Get Bread for the Workers," and "Our Families are Starving on the Land." The common people of Petrograd were ready to revolt, and were looking for leadership.

Lenin worked furiously to build an organization that would carry the next revolt into socialism. He planned a conference of factory committees; significantly, the Bolsheviks dealt directly with the workers. Always before they had used middlemen—labor groups or the Soviet. The conference, which opened on May 30, represented the proletariat as no previous group had. Lenin developed the slogan "Worker Control." Of its 421 members, 335 voted for the Bolsheviks, and it resolved to organize a Petrograd Center for all factory committees and trade unions. The factory committee had always been the workers' first recourse in time of protest; the new center united all such committees in Petrograd. As a means of hearing workers' grievances and shaping their views, it could hardly be overestimated.

Moreover, Lenin was working simultaneously to get more Bolsheviks into the Workers' Section of the Soviet. The first All-Russian Congress of Soviets* opened in Petrograd on June 3. Everyone wondered what sort of showing the Bolsheviks would make. There were 820 voting delegates, and the Bolsheviks claimed 105 of the 777 party-affiliated. It was a huge gain for them. And by now they virtually controlled the Workers' Section, so that with the Factory Committee Center, they reached all of Petrograd's proletariat.

Of course Lenin attended the Congress. And when the Menshevik minister Irakli Tsereteli said, "There is no political party in Russia which would, at the present time, say 'give us power'. . . ," Lenin shouted, "There is!" The delegates took this as a joke, but Lenin made it official in his speech. He was allowed only 15 minutes, which for a speaker of his type was barely time to introduce his topic. However, he stunned his listeners with a flat declaration of Bolshevik confidence in Bolshevik ability:

* There had been an earlier All-Russian Congress of Soviets at the end of March, before Lenin's return to Russia, but this second Congress is usually called the First.

The Citizen [a slur] Minister of Posts and Telegraphs . . . has
declared that there is no political party in Russia that would
consent to take the whole power on itself. I reply: there is . . .
No party can refuse, all parties are struggling and must struggle
for power, and our party will not refuse . . . [it]. Every moment
it is ready to take total power.*

He outlined what the Bolsheviks would do, given the opportunity. First, "arrest the largest capitalists, blast all their intrigues. Without this all phrases about a world without annexations and indemnities are empty words. Our second step would
be to declare to nations independently of their governments
that we consider all capitalists to be robbers. . . ." Lenin di-
gressed into name-calling, and had time to mention only one
other important aim, ending the war. Very few took him seriously. Most believed that the Bolsheviks would be pleased to
take power, but few, including the Bolshevik leadership, believed that they could cope with Russia's problems. The general feeling among non-Bolsheviks was that Bolsheviks were
very good at disrupting, disorganizing, and tearing down, but
no good at all at unifying, organizing, and building. Outside his
party, Lenin had few allies.

But one uncommited socialist was to prove of incalculable
importance in the days ahead. Trotsky had come home. He
had been in Brooklyn, New York, at the outbreak of the revolution, and while trying to get back to Russia had been interned
in Halifax, Nova Scotia, so that he had only arrived on May 4.
Although he was not a Bolshevik, he recognized in Lenin the
man who would make a revolution while others merely talked
about it, and he was ready to support him. Trotsky comple-
mented Lenin marvelously well. Brilliant where Lenin was
dogged; hot-blooded and emotional where Lenin was cool,
calm, and collected; Trotsky was the kind of orator the Russian
people loved, and a natural leader. He had enormous influence

* Sukhanov, *Zapiski o Revoliutsii,* 4:232.

with the soldiers, especially. Lenin stood aloof from Trotsky's emotional approach, but recognized his genius and gave him every opportunity to use it. (Lenin, unlike Tsar Nicholas, was never afraid of having brilliant men in his administration.) Trotsky, in return, developed a respect for Lenin that amounted almost to reverence, and lasted throughout his life.

Trotsky was not a modest man, but even so, he never put himself above Lenin in importance. He wrote that if Lenin had not been in Petrograd there could have been no October Revolution because the Bolshevik leaders "would have prevented it from occurring—of this I have not the slightest doubt! If Lenin had not been in Petersburg, I doubt whether I could have managed to conquer [their] . . . resistance. . . ." He could very well doubt. If Lenin had not been in Petrograd, Trotsky would not even have been attracted to the Bolsheviks; by May 4, when he returned, they would have been reunited with the Mensheviks and supporting the Provisional Government. And as a nonparty man, he would have had no influence with the leaders. Trotsky's great oratorical powers and his ability to work well under pressure—and in the middle of a mob—were very useful with the rank and file, but it took the cool determination of Lenin to scheme the leaders into his camp.

In those days Lenin hardly slept; he was everywhere at once, engaged in his own form of political activity. Sukhanov wrote,

Lenin behaved very exclusively, as if nobody were greater—like a great aristocrat. He was never seen at meetings of the Soviet, nor in the lobbies; as usual he was somewhere in the "underground," in intimate party circles. And when he appeared at a meeting he would demand the floor out of turn, disturbing the agenda. . . . To wait for the floor was against his principles.*

Lenin had no time to wait for the floor, or to listen to interminable speeches. The years in exile had made him his own

* *Ibid.,* 4:166.

best worker, and in Petrograd there was limitless opportunity
to work. By the third week of May, personal agitation had
gained him the allegiance of the First Machine Gun Regiment,
for example. They showed their strength when Second Lieuten-
ant Semashko—a Bolshevik—was arrested at the end of May.
The entire regiment, in full formation, invaded the commandant's headquarters, freed Semashko, and carried him out on
their shoulders. The Bolsheviks were building military power.

In June, Sukhanov wrote that

> For a long time now the Bolshevik military organization had
> worked successfully under the careful control of Lenin. This
> organ . . . was not limited to propaganda and agitation; it had
> succeeded in spreading a fairly good organization network not
> only over the capital, but in the provinces and at the front.*

Even junior officers were being won over, and now the Bolsheviks could count on many units: the Moscow Regiment, the
Grenadiers, the First Reserve Regiment, the Pavlovsky Regiment, the Michael Artillery School (heavy armaments), and
others. Almost all the committed military was now pro-Bolshevik. The others, except for two or three regiments, were neutral. So, since his return in April, Lenin had managed to trans-
fer the dependence of workers and soldiers on the Soviet to
dependence on the Bolsheviks. The Bolsheviks had become the
workers' and soldiers' new middlemen. Not only did a worker
who wanted to reach the Soviet now go through the Bolsheviks,
but when the Soviet wanted to reach the workers, it had to do
it through the Bolsheviks.

The importance of this arrangement was soon illustrated. At
the evening session of the All-Russian Congress of Soviets on
June 9, an emergency statement was read: a special assembly
of workers' delegates announced that an armed demonstration
against the Provisional Government was scheduled for the next

* *Ibid.*, 4:289.

day. The Workers' Center had been busy; that day, proclamations signed by the Bolshevik Central Committee and the
Central Bureau of the Factory Committees had been posted
throughout the working-class districts. They urged workers to
participate in "a peaceful demonstration against the counterrevolution at two o'clock on June 10." But the proclamation's
wording was terse and inflammatory. Its slogans were "Down
with the Tsarist Duma," "Down with the Ten Capitalist Ministers," "All Power to the All-Russian Soviet of Workers', Soldiers',
and Peasants' Deputies," "Long Live the Control and Organization of Industry," "End the War," "Neither a Separate Peace
with Wilhelm nor Secret Treaties with the French and British
Capitalists," "Bread, Peace, and Freedom." They were Lenin's
ideas boiled down to slogans.

What concerned non-Bolsheviks most was that the army
was to be part of the demonstration. Several regiments, including the First Machine Gun, intended to turn out armed. But
many provincial delegates to the congress were mystified; what
was all the fuss about? They hadn't come all the way to Petrograd to cope with local problems; it wasn't the congress' business. Petrograd ought to be used to demonstrations; as Sukhanov had said, everyone was demonstrating who wasn't too lazy.
This was a matter for the Petrograd Soviet, if it merited anyone's attention. But the fact was that the Petrograd Soviet was
powerless to reach the people except through the Bolsheviks,
and was calling on the congress because it didn't know what
else to do.

If the Soviet had lost control of the people, the Provisional
Government, before and after the coalition, had never had any
control to lose. Now it could only urge that everyone remain
calm. It promised to "suppress any attempts at violence with
all the strength of the State," which everyone knew wasn't
promising much. It was left to the congress to manage, in typical Russian fashion. (All important business seems to have
been transacted at night. This session began after midnight.)

The Soviet banned street meetings and proclamations for the next three days. Then its delegates went out to try to reach potential demonstrators—to the factories, barracks, and other places where revolutionaries congregated. All were to meet back at the Tauride Palace at eight in the morning, to compare notes.

Everyone knew what the Soviet was doing—whistling in the dark—but no one knew what the Bolsheviks were doing. Those at the congress seemed uncertain themselves; it was Bolshevik policy to decide on a line and then support it unanimously. The confusion and general demeanor of the Bolsheviks seemed to indicate that they had not yet reached agreement. But when the roving delegates met back at the Tauride on the morning of June 10, they discovered that the Bolshevik Central Committee had canceled the demonstration. What would have happened otherwise was a matter for conjecture; all the delegates who had gone out into Petrograd reported that they had found the people hostile. Sukhanov wrote that this was the moment that the Soviet should have made an all-out effort to win back the workers, but "Alas! . . . Having overcome their panic and plucked up their courage, the Menshevik-SR leaders flung themselves into an offensive against the Bolsheviks."

They formed a special commission and censured the Bolsheviks, calling their action a "political adventure" and advocating that in future no demonstrations be allowed except by approval of the Soviet. (Inasmuch as the Bolsheviks were a minority, this would bar them from demonstrating, but only temporarily—Lenin was working hard to build Bolshevik strength in the Soviet, and was succeeding.) Kamenev answered for the Bolsheviks; his defense was injured innocence. He said that a peaceful demonstration had been scheduled at a time when everyone was demonstrating, and that when the Congress, for reasons best known to itself, had requested a cancellation, the demonstration had immediately been canceled. Where was there any illegality or disloyalty in that?

The Menshevik Tsereteli couldn't control himself. He leaped to his feet and forecast coming events; he said that the Bolsheviks were conspiring to seize power and would continue to do so, and that they must be disarmed. (He didn't say how.) There was pandemonium in the meeting. The Bolsheviks left in a body, protesting noisily. Someone who had heard too many emotional speeches after sleepless nights was shrieking. The delegates split into two camps, one attacking the Bolsheviks and the other, Tsereteli. For three days they met and argued, and finally decided to call an all-city peaceful demonstration for June 18, with slogans common to all parties.

The Bolsheviks had been let off lightly, not because the majority thought them innocent, but because no one knew what else to do. But Tsereteli had been right; Lenin was plotting a Bolshevik takeover by a route which had to succeed; he was encouraging people to do what they already wanted to do, but to do it his way. All the potential ruling groups in Russia had been playing dog-in-the-manger with power. They didn't want it, but they didn't want anyone else to get it. The fact was that if some person or group did not set up machinery to cope with the nation's physical problems soon, there would be local civil wars all over Russia. Lenin didn't have to seize power, he had only to build a strong enough following so that when he picked up the power that the others had dropped, no one would be able to take it away from him. So while the other leaders made speeches in the Soviet, or in the Provisional Government, Lenin worked with the common people.

The June 18 demonstration grew out of the Soviet leaders' conviction that if the people wanted to demonstrate they would, and that it was better to plan the time and place and bless the event than to admit that the Provisional Government and Soviet were powerless. The Soviet also believed that if they backed it, the turnout would show majority support for the causes of unification and conciliation. In any case, it could do nothing more—it had no organization to reach the masses.

The Bolsheviks had such an organization, and worked day and night to rouse supporters and gain converts. The demonstration, when it came, was overwhelmingly Bolshevik. Soviet banners were lost in a sea of "Down with the Ten Capitalist Ministers" and other Bolshevik slogans. In spite of the crowd— 400,000 marched—it was a peaceful demonstration; and the government decided to take no official notice of Bolshevik strength, seeing to it that the big newspapers reported the event as a government victory. But the people who had marched knew who had been there, and Bolshevik power continued to grow. On July 2, at an all-city conference of the Interdistrict party, the Interdistrictites examined the program of the Bolshevik party and adopted it with only a few minor amendments.

7. The July Days

July was hot, for Petrograd, and the goodwill that had distinguished the early months of the revolution was giving way to bad temper. The Provisional Government and the Soviet were both torn by internal dissension and their members were unable to agree on anything practical. Living conditions were growing worse, and the people were being given nothing but promises. While the leaders argued, a new crisis was brewing across town. It seems to have started when members of the Petrograd garrison were ordered to the front. Bolshevik agitators had warned all soldiers that counterrevolutionary forces might attempt to remove them from the city. The soldiers suspected a bourgeois plot. The First Machine Gun Regiment decided that it would send a few units and that the others would demonstrate. Other regiments joined the demonstrators, as did thousands of workers and the Red Guard (armed workers).

Lenin had not planned this; he was in Finland when it began. His party got word to him the same day, and he started back at once, arriving on the fourth. In the meantime, the Kadet ministers had resigned in a body, and the Coalition Cabinet had, in falling, proclaimed that the coalition should be replaced with a "wholly democratic government made up of Soviet parties." They were trying to hand the government to the Soviet. While the Soviet tried to find a suitable way to refuse this gift of power, the workers and soldiers took to the streets. The Soviet appealed to the Bolshevik delegates, who, after meeting during the day, agreed to go to factories and barracks, to try to calm the demonstrators. But then they changed their minds. Kamanev explained that the Bolsheviks hadn't called the demonstration, but that since the masses clearly wanted to demonstrate, the party thought it should organize them and support them. If the Bolsheviks had not ordered the demonstration, they were at least going to try to lead it.

Meanwhile, crowds surged through Petrograd, which began to look as it had in February. This was not an organized political group now; it was a potential mob. Regiments marched imposingly, but without orders or destinations. Crowds milled about, but seemed to congregate more at the Soviet's Tauride Palace than at the government's Marian. They had had high hopes of the Soviet, but nothing had come from it, and they were angry in their disappointment. There were cries that the executive committee should be arrested, but it was not clear who should do the arresting. It was all shouting and empty gesture, and by that night the demonstration seemed to be petering out, except for a futile and confused foray in which two groups fired on each other with machine guns, without seeming to know why.

A joint session of the Soviet's Central Executive Committee opened after midnight. The members argued among themselves till dawn. The Bolsheviks were also meeting; whereas the Soviet was considering ways and means to end the uprising, the Bolsheviks had an even more complicated decision to make: should they try to take over the demonstration, and if they did, where would they lead it? Was it time for a Bolshevik coup? Were they strong enough yet? If they risked all, they might lose all. Most of the leaders were apprehensive.

The next morning the mob was out again. Streetcars weren't

running and many stores were closed. The Soviet delegates, who'd been up all night, were not at their best. Then, at ten in the morning, a contingent of about 20,000 sailors, soldiers, and workers arrived from Kronstadt. The big naval base was there, and about 40 ships had brought what looked like every able-bodied male. The Bolsheviks had called the base for support earlier, when they had contemplated taking over the demonstration, but the Kronstadters had arrived at a very awkward time. At Kshesinskaya's Palace, they waited for instructions. Lenin came out onto the balcony and made the same sort of speech he'd been making since April—he denounced the Provisional Government and the "social-traitors" of the Soviet. He called for the defense of the revolution and for loyalty to the Bolsheviks. What he did not do was give specific directions to 20,000 emotional people who'd made, they thought, a voyage of rescue.

It was an anticlimax for the Kronstadters, and a dangerous situation, since men keyed up to fight will usually find a cause. Sukhanov wrote that firing began at about noon, but that it was the result of hysterical tension rather than plan. ". . . As a rule it began with a chance shot; panic would follow; rifles began to go off at random. There were dead and wounded everywhere." It was hard to know what side anyone was on. Violence mounted, and pogroms and looting began. Then, as it seemed that terror would devastate the city, the skies opened and it began to pour. Witnesses said that the demonstrators ran from the raindrops as if they had been bullets. But the Kronstadters had no homes in Petrograd to run to, and at 5:00 P.M. they converged on the Tauride Palace, wet and furious. They wanted to know why, when the Kadets had virtually thrust the power at the Soviet, the socialists had refused it. Victor Chernov, the Menshevik leader, was "taken into custody" by the mob, and it took all of Trotsky's skill of persuasion to get him free and to safety.

For the Soviet delegates, it was like a nightmare come true.

And it wasn't over; at about 7.00 P.M. the 176th Reserve
Regiment arrived from Krasnoe Selo "to defend the revolution." This was one of the Bolshevik's rallying phrases. Lately,
it translated "to destroy the Coalition Government and the
non-Bolshevik members of the Soviet," but no one had explained that to the soldiers. What happened next typifies the
complications of the Revolution. Fyodor Ilyich Dan, a Menshevik leader, didn't know that the soldiers had been called by
the Bolsheviks and were a "mutinous group." He went out to
welcome them and told them that they'd arrived just in time to
defend the revolution, which in *his* translation meant to save the
Executive Committee of the Soviet. He then put the soldiers on
sentry duty—in effect, guarding the palace against their own
side. Sukhanov wrote,

> Dan didn't know what this regiment was for and why it had
> come. But Dan found a use for the regiment. And the regiment
> didn't know what it was supposed to do when it reached the
> end of its journey. And not receiving other orders it unquestion-
> ingly put itself into the service of the enemy. Now the business
> was all over. The regiment was dispersed, the minds of the
> soldiers hopelessly confused. It was already impossible to turn
> them into a fighting force again.*

Next, the horrified executive committee was invaded by
about 40 armed workers, a handful of the 30,000 from the
Putilov Works who had just arrived at the Tauride. One of
them leaped onto the speaker's platform and almost hysterically
accused the group of betraying the working class by refusing to
take and use power. Chkheidze, "under whose nose the rifle
was dancing about," spoke soothingly, and gave the man a
manifesto—one of those printed the night before. It said that
everyone who didn't go home peaceably was a traitor to the
revolution, and so was meaningless, but having it thrust into

---

* Sukhanov, *Zapiski o Revoliutsii,* 4:429.

his hand seemed to break the spell for the worker, who allowed himself to be led out. Luckily, the workers had been caught in the rain on the way to the palace, and soon went home to get dry. Most of the Kronstadters had also taken ship for home, but two or three thousand had stayed in the area near Bolshevik headquarters, just in case. These few thousand later decided to seize and occupy Peter-Paul Fortress, and did so. Once inside, they didn't know what to do with their new acquisition, but armed themselves from its arsenal and waited. The Soviet later reclaimed the fortress without bloodshed.

The political part of the demonstration had fizzled out. Mobs still rampaged through the city—400 people were killed or wounded before the last were dispersed—but their excesses were riots, not political demonstrations. In combating the uprising, the politicians had been able to think of nothing practical except to play on the peasants' fears of atheists and traitors, and to call the Bolsheviks both. Sukhanov says that the Soviet "could not explain its theories to the peasants but it wasn't so difficult to scare them with Lenin and anarchy." Most of the soldiers were peasants.

The Soviet was still sitting, but about an hour before midnight, it broke for food and rest, and heard that new "evidence" of Lenin's connection with the German general staff was to be published the next day. In spite of its distrust of Lenin, no one in the Soviet believed he would betray his ideals for any incentive, much less money, and it says much for the basic honesty of the Mensheviks that they worked hard to defend him from such charges, knowing that he would destroy them if he got the chance.

The Provisional Government was less high-minded; the minister of justice, Pereverzev, had already ordered that *Pravda* be shut down. A detachment had taken the staff by surprise, arresting everyone in the printing shop and offices, and confiscating all materials. When the place stood empty, a mob of "war wounded" and Black Hundreds destroyed the editorial offices, smashing and burning everything. The Bolshevik Central Committee met all night. Sukhanov said, "This was a difficult night for them. *Pravda* was smashed up; slandering of Lenin had taken unprecedented form; the movement for which they had taken responsibility was collapsing quite ignominously." Sukhanov went to a friend's house to nap; there he found the prominent Bolshevik Anatoli Vasilievich Lunacharsky bedded down on two chairs. Lunacharsky was terribly depressed, according to Sukhanov, and told him that

> on the night of July 4 . . . Lenin definitely had a plan to overturn the government. To all intents and purposes, power was to be transferred into the hands of the Bolshevik Central Committee, although officially it would be embodied in a soviet ministry of prominent and popular Bolsheviks. For the present, three ministers would be nominated: Lenin, Trotsky, and Lunacharsky. This government would immediately promulgate decrees about peace and land, thus attracting all the sympathies of the millions of the masses of the capital and the provinces and consolidating their own power. An agreement of this kind was made among Lenin, Trotsky, and Lunacharsky. It was subscribed to at the time that the Kronstadters were making their way . . . to the Tauride Palace. The coup would happen thus: the 176th Regiment arriving from Krasnoe Selo, the same which Dan had placed on guard as sentries in the Tauride Palace, would arrest the Central Executive Committee. At the same time Lenin would arrive at the scene of action and proclaim the new power. But Lenin was late. The 176th Regiment was intercepted and became disorganized. The revolution did not succeed.*

Later, Trotsky and Lunacharsky both discredited this story. It does not sound like Lenin, but if anything would lend credence to it, it is People's Commissar Lunacharsky's refutation, written on March 30, 1920. It is seven paragraphs long, but its gist is:

* Sukhanov, *Zapiski o Revoliutsii,* 4:511–512.

. . . you have fallen into profound error, which for you, as for history, may have unpleasant consequences. . . . Certainly neither Comrade Lenin, nor Comrade Trotsky, much less myself, had come to an agreement to seize power.

The July Days had only this meaning . . . which we advanced with perfect openness: All power to the Soviet of Workers', Soldiers', and Peasants' Deputies.*

In any case, the Bolsheviks maintained that the July Days had been completely spontaneous, and that they, the Bolsheviks, had only tried to contain the demonstrations and keep them peaceful. Internal evidence seems to suggest that the demonstrations did indeed start spontaneously, and that they were fueled by rank-and-file agitators without instructions from Bolshevik leaders. The fact that the leaders were caught unawares, with Lenin out of the country, meant that they made hasty decisions which were later reversed. Certainly the Bolsheviks had not shown the organization that was a hallmark of Lenin's leadership. Lenin, brought in late, was trying to decide what his strength would allow. This would explain his behavior with the Kronstadters: he tried to calm them until he could decide how best to use them, knowing that he would want their revolutionary zeal, if not that day, then someday soon.

There was certainly no way of proving that the Bolsheviks had been responsible for the July Days. But the bourgeoisie decided that this was an opportunity to discredit them once and for all, and to destroy Lenin. The papers resurrected the charges of his spying for the Germans, this time with "proof"— documents which purported to prove that money and instructions were being sent from Germany via Stockholm, and that the Germans had ordered Lenin to lead an insurrection—the July Days—in order to weaken Russia. The socialists, even those who detested the Bolsheviks, closed ranks to refute what they were sure was a false accusation.

* *Ibid.,* 4:514–515.

The Soviet and the Provisional Government ordered the newspapers to hold the material till an investigation could be made, but one paper printed it anyway, and the next day, according to Sukhanov, the "whole bourgeois gutter press" had the story. He felt that no one could possibly have credited the slander—the two informants were notoriously anti-Lenin—except for the timing. Juxtaposed against the July Days, it seemed credible to many. The bourgeoisie believed it because it would have believed anything of Lenin, and the proletariat believed it because of Lenin's strangely indecisive behavior during the demonstrations. The people were waiting to be led, and couldn't understand why, one after another, all their natural leaders had rejected the power offered them. The same emotion that had brought the hysterical workers to the Soviet's executive committee now turned against the Bolsheviks, and the people spoke bitterly of betrayal.

It was one of those few times when socialist leaders found themselves defending Lenin while the people demanded his scalp. In the Tauride, left-wingers were protesting furiously the fact (which they had just discovered) that during the July Days troops had been summoned from the front to "pacify" Petrograd, when the Bolshevik Grigori Evseyevich Zinoviev dashed in, pleading for help. He said that the Soviet would have to make every effort to refute the slander and clear Lenin's name. Then he hurried off; he was meeting Lenin, who had gone underground that morning—the 5th.

On the 6th Lenin and Zinoviev were hidden by the Caucasian Bolshevik whose daughter later married Stalin. On the seventh, the order for Lenin's arrest appeared; he shaved his beard, got a wig, and prepared to move on. He and Zinoviev went into hiding at Razliv, where they stayed till August 8. They posed as Finnish laborers, hired for the summer. Emelyanov, their host, worked in the strongly Bolshevik Sestroretzk Arms Factory, but like most workers still had one foot on the land. The Emelyanovs' farm became a Bolshevik headquarters;

it was only 20 miles from Petrograd, and Bolshevik leaders came and went constantly. Lenin had an outdoor "office"—two logs—where he was writing *The State and Revolution*.

The State and Revolution is oddly anarchistic. Generally speaking, Lenin was an administrator by natural inclination; he had no use for anarchy. But this book's central idea is, "while the state exists there will be no freedom. Where there is freedom there will be no state." Like all of Lenin's works, it is a "how-to" book. It tells how to make a revolution and how to administer society afterward. It is the Communists' guidebook. But while they followed the first half, and while the book does project a socialist dictatorship for an indefinite period, the government which Lenin actually set up bore little resemblance to the government projected in the book, partly because class distinctions refused to disappear as Lenin had predicted they would. The old elite was outlawed, but a new one emerged.

Meanwhile, in Petrograd, the Bolshevik party was in deep trouble. By nightfall on July 5, Sukhanov said, "They were arresting in the street anyone who said a word in favor of the Bolsheviks. It was no longer possible to say that Lenin was an honest man; you'd be arrested." Kshesinskaya's Palace was deserted. Black Hundreds prowled the city, arresting anarchists and Bolsheviks, and some of yesterday's Bolsheviks went over to their side. (Agitators often did not stress party or philosophy, they simply encouraged performance of certain activities. It was not inconsistent for peasant-soldiers who had rampaged for the Bolsheviks now to rampage for the rightists. Moreover, the peasants were traditionally anti-Semitic, as were the Black Hundreds, and now, in need of a scapegoat, they were vulnerable to arguments which played on their prejudice.) Rightist power began to engulf even the Soviet.

On the 6th Kerensky returned from the front and went straight to the session of the Provisional Government. He arrived at about 9:00 P.M. The government had already decided to arrest all the instigators of the July Days, but Kerensky insisted that Lenin be arrested at once. (He also wanted all army units that had taken part in the revolt to be disbanded and reassigned at the discretion of the minister of war—himself.) Dramatically, the militia appeared at Lenin's old apartment at two in the morning, but of course he was long gone.

Sukhanov said that many, including himself, were shocked at Lenin's flight. They disapproved because it seemed wrong-headed—there was no danger of harsh sentencing, such as exile, and it left the Bolshevik masses without their leader at a very difficult time. Sukhanov said that Lenin could have led the party from jail, and that his arrest would have strengthened his followers and united them, adding that many Bolsheviks—and Trotsky—were in jail for six weeks to two months, where "with martyrs' halos they served as an inexhaustible source of agitation against the government of Kerensky and Tsereteli." Sukhanov could not understand how Lenin could bear to run without first being sure that the charges of treason had been refuted. "Any other mortal would have demanded justice and an investigation. ... Any other would have done all that was necessary for rehabilitation personally, with maximum energy. But Lenin proposed that others, his opponents, do this. And he sought to save himself by escaping and hiding. In the whole world only Lenin would act this way."*

But Sukhanov was sure the charges were completely unfounded. Lenin, on the other hand, may have felt that while he was morally innocent of having betrayed his country, he would never be able to prove it, since he had actually taken German money. Certainly he had been receiving money from somewhere to build the party; dues alone could not have begun to finance his activities. In April the Bolsheviks had had only 49,000 members, and few of them were in a position to make large donations, even if they had wanted to. But during the next few months, the party had produced and distributed liter-

* Sukhanov, *Zapiski o Revoliutsii,* 4:482.

ally tons of literature and agitation, and had employed full-time agitators and propagandists, and all of this required money. Moreover, the German government's adviser on subversion was Dr. Alexander Israel Helphand* who had been a member of the Russian Social Democratic party. He was acquainted with Lenin and had been a close associate of Trotsky. Helphand had been in Germany when the war broke out, and had grown rich as middleman in the distribution of huge sums to sponsor subversion in Russia. It would have been odd if he had not approached Lenin, and it would have been very unlike Lenin to reject money for the Bolsheviks. German money he would have put in the party treasury and German instructions he would have ignored. Certainly he had not ordered the July Days at the suggestion of the Germans; the "evidence" for this accusation was later proved to be a forgery. In any case, Lenin's idea of useful activity was quite unlike Sukhanov's, and he was much less interested in defending his honor than in making a revolution.

At the end of the first week in July, it must have seemed that Kerensky and the Provisional Government had beaten Lenin. On July 7, Lenin was in flight and Kerensky became premier, thus satisfying a long-held ambition. (He remained war minister as well.) He was even to utilize lost battles. On the sixth, the Russian army at the front had been severely defeated; the official communiques blamed Bolshevik agitation. Several reactionary rulings resulted: the death penalty, which had been abolished in the army, was reimposed. There were new restrictions on public meetings and on the press.

Antileftist feelings ran high; the Second Coalition worked to disarm not only the mutinous regiments, but also the revolutionary citizenry, including the Red Guards. (Trotsky wrote that they hid their best weapons, turning in only those that were ancient or broken.) The order was out to arrest all Bolshe-

---

* Helphand's name sometimes appears as "Gelfand" or "Helfand"; socialists often called him by the pseudonym "Parvus."

viks. But the new government lacked the police apparatus of the old tsarist regime, and its leaders seemed to share the delusion that once a thing was down on paper, it was accomplished. Most of the ordinary members escaped arrest, but on July 22, Trotsky and Lunacharsky were imprisoned. The antirevolutionaries, unable to identify rank-and-file party members, concentrated on leaders. Military cadets "executed a raid on the government Mensheviks themselves, whose party was headed by the minister of the interior. Was this excessive?" asks Sukhanov ironically. "But it was completely compatible with the general mood and particularly with the tone of the bourgeois press."

By July 23, Kerensky had chosen a bourgeois cabinet. On the next day a new government was formed—the Third Coalition. Kerensky kept the army and navy for himself, and parceled the other portfolios among right-wing SRs and Kadets. It looked as though the Bolshevik party had been a victim of the July Days.

8. "The Worse it is, the Better it is"

The Third Coalition produced no changes. The politicians went on talking, while living conditions in Petrograd continued to deteriorate. Food was scrace, and the bread ration, which had started at one and one-half pounds a day, was dropping; before the food supply improved, it would be down to a quarter of a pound a day, provided that the buyer could find it for sale and afford the price. Profiteering was common. Nor was food the only necessity rationed; clothing and fuel were equally scarce. Even electricity was in short supply. The city turned on the current only from 6:00 P.M. till midnight, and most of the streets were unlit. (Fear of German Zeppelins, as well as economy, was a consideration here.) Candles cost about 40 cents apiece, and kerosene was very hard to get.

As rationing became more stringent, queues lengthened. People lined up before dawn, as night workers and revelers were going home. Petrograd's theaters, opera house, film houses, ballet, and other entertainment centers were open seven nights a week, and were well-attended. But no one was doing anything for the poor people. No one tried to fill the void left by the Bolsheviks' downfall—except the Bolsheviks. They had regrouped and were publishing again. They had even settled into new headquarters in the Smolny Institute, formerly a convent

91

school for young ladies. It was a huge building, 200 yards long and three stories high. Bolsheviks entering by the main door passed under a huge stone carving of the imperial arms, but now the chaste white rooms—there were more than 100—were full of hurrying revolutionaries, and the old dining room served a very different kind of meal: cabbage soup and black bread was the typical Bolshevik menu, with tea served in tin cups.

On July 26 the Bolsheviks even managed to hold their Sixth Congress. The leaders were unable to attend, but the party was used to that, and their recent troubles had united the membership more strongly than ever. They numbered 240,000 now, as against 50,000 in April. Moreover, 41,000 of these members were from Petrograd and 50,000 were from Moscow. Whoever could take the capitals could cope with the countryside afterward. The congress lasted a week, and 270 delegates attended, so obviously the arresting of Bolsheviks was a haphazard affair. And delegates from the provinces raised everyone's spirits with the assurance that the July Days had scarcely been noticed outside Petrograd. After the congress, the Workers' Section of the Petrograd Soviet set up its own Praesidium, with Bolshevik members. And when the Second Conference of Factory Committees opened on August 7, it too was Bolshevik. The upper classes hardly noticed.

In spite of polarization, upper and lower classes still passed each other on the streets of Petrograd, and to the old contrasts were added new contrasts. The royal emblems had all been defaced or obliterated, but the upper classes still observed the table of ranks, and wore appropriate uniforms. The tsarist statues now held little red flags in their cast iron hands, but young ladies still came from the provinces to "be finished," and middle class women took tea together in the afternoons, except that now each brought her own bread and sugar. They "wished that the tsar were back, or that the Germans would come or anything that would solve the servant problem," John Reed wrote.

Reed* lived among the upper classes during this period. He wrote,

> A large section of the propertied classes preferred the Germans to the Revolution—even to the Provisional Government—and didn't hesitate to say so. In the Russian household where I lived the subject of conversation at the dinnertable was almost invariably the coming of the Germans, bringing "law and order". . . . One evening I spent at the house of a Moscow merchant; during tea we asked the eleven people at the table whether they preferred "Wilhelm or the Bolsheviki." The vote was ten to one for Wilhelm.†

They expressed the same idea publicly. Mikhail Rodzianko, leader of the Kadets' right wing, wrote in *Utro Rosii* that it would be just as well if the Germans took Petrograd, because they would destroy the revolutionary organization. He said that the revolutionaries would bring "nothing but disaster" to Russia, and added that he'd have no regrets if the Baltic Fleet were destroyed too, for the same reason.

But if the classes were polarized by the revolution, their practical reactions were similar: they talked. Everyone debated. Reed wrote,

> . . . in theatres, circuses, school-houses, clubs, Soviet meeting rooms, Union headquarters, barracks . . . in the trenches at the Front, in village squares, factories. . . . For months in Petrograd and all over Russia every street-corner was a public tribune. In railway trains, street cars, always the spurting up of an impromptu debate. . . . There were always three or four conventions

---

* John Reed was an American journalist sent to Russia to cover the revolution. He was an uncritical supporter of the revolution and of Lenin, expecting the best of both.

† John Reed, *Ten Days that Shook the World* (New York: Boni and Liveright, 1919), p. 8. Reprinted by permission of International Publishers Co., Inc.

going on in Petrograd. At every meeting, attempts to limit the time of speakers [were] voted down.*

Krupskaya was struck by the same phenomenon:

> The streets at that time presented an interesting sight; everywhere groups gathered, heatedly discussing the political situation and all the events that occurred. I used to mingle with the crowd and listen. Once I walked three hours . . . so interesting were these meetings. There was a courtyard opposite our house from which excited arguments could be heard when we opened the window at night. . . . At one o'clock in the morning disjointed words could be heard such as: Bolsheviks, Mensheviks. . . . At three o'clock; Miluykov, Bolsheviks. . . . At five o'clock the same; politics and meetings. The white nights of Petrograd are now always associated in my mind with these nightly meetings.†

While the people talked, the leaders talked. Kerensky had decided to call a State Conference of every political and special-interest group in Russia. Lenin denounced the idea, and the Bolsheviks did not attend. The conference was to open in Moscow on August 12; Kerensky had chosen Moscow because he thought it less revolutionary than Petrograd. General Lavr Georgievich Kornilov, the army's commander in chief, had been invited to address the delegates on opening day and to report on the military situation. But Kornilov had other plans for the trip; he was preparing a rightist coup. He had stationed four cavalry divisions near Petrograd to be used when the time was right. Meanwhile, he went to Moscow by train. The crowd assembled to greet him at the station watched while the Tekintsi, the Savage Division honor guard, leapt from the train; with their long red coats and curved swords they made an impressive sight. They formed two rows on the platform, and Kornilov reviewed them. Ladies threw flowers and wept. A Kadet wel-

---

* *Ibid.,* pp. 14–15.
† Krupskaya, *Reminiscences of Lenin,* pp. 216–217.

come ended, "Save Russia and a grateful people will reward you!" Finally, officers carried the general out on their shoulders. His followers distributed his biography (with portrait) throughout the city, from automobiles.

Kornilov might have noticed that the whole of Moscow was in the grip of a general strike—the workers' reaction to the State Conference. As Sukhanov noted, "The whole working class was following the Bolsheviks against its own Soviet!" The Conference seethed with the suspicions of each faction for the others. Kerensky's speech promised that any attempts against the new government would be put down with blood and iron, but since any "iron" available was either in the hands of the Bolsheviks or the Kornilovites, this impressed no one. When Kornilov spoke, the leftists thought he implied that he would throw Petrograd to the Germans if that was the only way to overthrow the revolution. However, he got a standing ovation, except from the soldiers, which again should have told him and his supporters something.

Kornilov was not noted for his intelligence. (A colleague had said that he had the heart of a lion and the brain of a sheep.) But to give him his due, he had been trained to pay no attention to the opinion of common soldiers, and his natural contacts were such that he assumed far greater support than he actually had. Officers of the army and navy, and most of the upper classes, would have supported him, as would the Allied ambassadors, whose main consideration was the fact that with him in charge, Russia would definitely stay in the war. (The war news was going from bad to worse; between August 18–21 the Germans broke through the northern front, captured Riga, and were thus in a position to threaten Petrograd.)

While Kornilov planned his coup, the Bolsheviks scored another victory. Elections to the Petrograd Town Council were scheduled for August 20. (Provisional delegates had been elected in May, but citywide direct elections were now to decide the official membership.) All parties were anticipating the elections, which would show who had the real power in the city. But almost no preelection agitation was evident; everyone was sick of agitation and demonstration. The politicians expected an apathetic turnout.

They were surprised. The voters were tired of meeting, but not of voting; 549,400 turned out. The Socialist Revolutionary party kept first place with 37 percent of the total vote, but in May they had had much more. The Kadets got about 20 percent of the vote, and the Mensheviks only 23,000 in all. Sukhanov wrote,

> Who was the principal and only victor . . . ? It was the Bolsheviks, so lately trampled in the mud, charged with treason and corruption, completely crushed morally and materially, filling the prisons of the capital up until that day. You see, it seemed they were destroyed, never to rise up again.
>
> The Bolsheviks in the August elections in the capital got just short of 200,000 votes, that is 33 percent. A third of Petersburg. Again, the whole proletariat of the capital.*

It was ironic that as his party gained power again, Lenin was on his way out of Russia. On August 21–22, acting as a stoker on a train, he crossed the border into Finland, where he continued to move from one hideout to another until he came to Helsingfors. There his protector was a Bolshevik sympathizer who was also, conveniently, the city's police chief.

The Bolsheviks' best piece of luck was still to come. Back in Russia, Kornilov was planning to take Petrograd. The news reached the capital on August 27, and leaders reacted according to their personalities: Kerensky, who had appointed Kornilov commander in chief, ordered him to surrender his command and report to him at once. Instead, Kornilov ordered his men to proceed to Petrograd. It was foolish of him; not one tsarist echelon had got through during the February Revolution,

---

* Sukhanov, *Zapiski o Revoliutsii,* 5:193.

and the rightists had had more power then. Kornilov's plan called for inciting the masses of Petrograd to riot, restoring law and order with his troops, and then retaining the power in a dictatorship under martial law.

As the Petrograd Soviet's members closed ranks against this new threat from the right, all fears of the Bolsheviks were forgotten. The Bolsheviks were elated. They reasoned that Kornilov hadn't a chance of succeeding, and that his attempt would prove to the workers that the Bolsheviks had been telling them the truth when they said that the bourgeoisie had no intention of allowing the masses to govern themselves. Also, rightist politicians would no longer be able to castigate the Bolsheviks for the July Days. They couldn't prove that that had been an attempted coup, and this clearly was.

In the Soviet, a right-wing Menshevik proposed that a defense committee be formed—ironically, in view of what came from his suggestion: the Military Revolutionary Committee. It didn't matter that Bolsheviks were few in the committee at first; the whole idea of having it was to raise an army; and to reach soldiers and workers who could be counted on to combat Kornilov, Bolshevik middlemen were necessary. The Military Revolutionary Committee was bound to become a Bolshevik tool, and even in its first day—it was formed on August 28— it showed how far a little practical work could go. It began with precautions for withstanding a siege, from digging trenches to making sure the food held out. The bread ration was cut again, this time to a half-pound a day. It also appealed to armaments workers, who put themselves on round-the-clock production. And it began distributing rifles to the Red Guards.

Meanwhile, on the night of August 27 and the morning of the 28th, the Central Executive Committee had issued a series of proclamations to the army soviets and committees, and to railroad, postal, and telegraph workers, informing them of Kornilov's intentions, and asking them to close all transportation and communication lines to him. The Bolsheviks organized meetings in all barracks and workers' districts. Everything was ready for Kornilov.

But Kornilov never came. When his soldiers left the front, they had thought they were going to fight the Germans beyond Riga. Later they had been told that Bolshevik agents for Germany had started riots in Petrograd, and that they were needed there to restore peace. But when the eight echelons reached Luga and talked with the garrison there, they heard a different story. Local agitators had documents to show that the general was moving against the legitimate government. The soldiers were bewildered, and not likely to go anywhere till they'd had some satisfactory answers.

One of Kornilov's main hopes was his Savage Division, Caucasian mountaineers who were famous for "not caring whom they killed." By 4:00 P.M. on August 28 the Savage Division was within 42 versts (less than 28 miles) of Petrograd, where they were stalled by cut train tracks. A reconnaissance detachment was sent out. Meanwhile, that morning, the Soviet's Central Executive Committee had sent a special delegation of Muslims and Caucasians, kinsmen of the Savage Division's members, to meet them. The delegation met the reconnaissance detachment of Kornilovites, who assured them safe conduct and escorted them back to their officers. The officers refused to let the delegation speak to the men of the division, but the members had already talked at length with the reconnaissance detachment, and word spread. The Savage Division refused to proceed. It would have been difficult in any case, with railway lines cut and supply trains diverted.

By the evening of August 28, all routes were closed to Kornilov. The trains wouldn't run for him, and the garrisons of surrounding towns were on the roads to see that he didn't pass. Postal and telegraph workers intercepted messages and handed them to the Military Revolutionary Committee. Everywhere, people demonstrated against Kornilov. Soldiers at the front arrested several generals whom they thought had collaborated in the attempted coup. And on September 1, Kornilov was arrested with his staff.

The Kornilov Rebellion was a Bolshevik miracle. Now everyone saw the July Days in a new light. The measures taken by rightists afterward—the shutting down of Bolshevik headquarters, the destruction of *Pravda*, the attack on Lenin—people now saw as a foreshadowing of the Kornilov coup. By mid-August, Bolshevik membership had doubled. On September 1, a Bolshevik resolution carried the Petrograd Soviet for the first time. The Bolsheviks demanded a new Praesidium (the governing board of the Soviet), and the delegates voted 519 for the resolution, 414 to retain the old Praesidium, with 67 abstentions. The Bolsheviks now controlled the Soviet. Bolshevik leaders were released from jail—Trotsky got out on bail on September 4, and became the Soviet's new president. (Lenin was still facing charges of treason, so he could not show himself.)

Kornilov had not only given the Bolsheviks the Soviet and discredited the Kerensky government,* but had prompted the formation of the Military Revolutionary Committee. It is impossible to overestimate the importance of the committee, not only in the capitals, but in the provinces, where the Bolsheviks were still weak. It fitted prefectly into Lenin's organizational pyramid, and supplied officers for the Bolshevik "army."

Bolshevik strength continued to grow. The Petrograd Soviet called for a Congress of Soviets, to be held on October 20. The Bolsheviks believed that such a Congress would be proof of new support in outlying areas, and they were right. At about this time, the Bolsheviks resurrected an old slogan: "All Power to the Soviet." Now they were referring to Bolshevik soviets. The bourgeois press was worried, but had been reporting

---

* A Democratic Conference had been held in Petrograd, September 14–21, to debate whether Russia should have another coalition or a wholly socialist government, and the Fourth Coalition emerged. The Third Coalition had lasted only two months, and during that time it had become clear that all the real power was in Bolshevik hands.

Lenin disguised as the worker K. P. Ivanov. This was the photograph on his false identity card when he went to Finland in August, 1917.

Bolshevik plots for so long that it had no new superlatives, now that it really saw one developing. In any case, the Fourth Coalition was powerless. It had no way of coping with anything except to issue directives and hope that they were followed.

9. Lenin Stands Alone

As the Bolsheviks consolidated their gains, Lenin made plans to return to Russia. The Central Committee, prompted no doubt by fears for his safety, forbade him to come out of hiding without its authorization. They may also have wanted to keep him at a safe distance. He was furious with them and had made his anger felt from Finland; what might he do in person? During his exile he had continually criticized the policy of the Central Committee as too conservative. (Lenin had always been to the left of Bolshevik leadership.) On August 20, *Pravda* had printed, without dissenting editorial comment, an article entitled "What Not To Do," which was against insurrection. Lenin had written an anonymous rebuttal at once. He had called various members of the committee to Finland and talked with them, but once back in Petrograd they had done as they liked, and what they seemed to like was the Soviet's daily routine—making speeches and drafting documents. Lenin wanted to see more action.

When the Democratic Conference opened on September 14, Lenin had written, "Our party has now at the Democratic Conference practically its own congress and this congress has got to decide (whether it wants to or not) the fate of the revolution." A few days later he had written:

We ought at once to solidify the Bolshevik faction at the Conference. . . draw up a short declaration . . . move our whole faction to the factories and barracks. At the same time without losing a minute we ought to organize a staff of insurrectionary detachments, deploy our forces, move the loyal regiments into the most important positions, surround the Alexandrinka [site of the conference], occupy Peter and Paul, arrest the General Staff and the government, send against the junkers and the Savage Division those detachments which are ready to die fighting, but not let the enemy advance to the center of the city; we ought to mobilize the armed workers, summon them to a desperate final battle, occupy the telegraph and telephone stations at once, install our insurrectionary staff at the central telephone station. . . .*

Lenin spelled it all out, but the Bolshevik Central Committee did none of these things. Instead, it watched while the government formed another do-nothing subgroup. This was the Provisional Council of the Russian Republic, better known as the Pre-Parliament. It was scheduled to meet October 7 in the Marian Palace. Lenin raged. He instructed the Bolsheviks to boycott the Pre-Parliament, but without success. The Bolshevik faction at the Conference rejected his proposal 70 to 50. No one in the Central Committee supported it. Four years later, Trotsky heard Nikolai Ivanovich Bukharin reminisce about this period. He said:

The letter [from Lenin] was written with extraordinary force and threatened us with all sorts of punishments. We all gasped. Nobody had yet posed the question so abruptly. At first all were bewildered. Afterward, having talked it over, we made a decision. Perhaps that was the sole case in the history of our party when the Central Committee unanimously decided to burn a letter by Lenin.†

The Central Committee was afraid to seize power. Its mem-

* Trotsky, *History of the Russian Revolution,* 3:132.
† *Ibid.,* 3:133.

bers knew they could take Petrograd, and that their forces
would probably prevail in Moscow, but what about the provinces? If they tried and lost, it would mean the end of the
party. Lenin was writing stinging letters; if the Soviet could
move against Kornilov, it could move against the government.
He said that the Central Committee was developing the bureau-
cratic habit of substituting conferences and proclamations for
action. When a list of Bolshevik candidates for the Constituent
Assembly was published at the end of September, Lenin was
exasperated. It contained too many intellectuals and too few
workers, he said. He propagandized constantly for insurrection,
saying, "In this matter, it is now impossible to be premature."
Nothing happened.

As usual, when Lenin got no cooperation from Bolshevik
leaders, he bypassed them and went straight to the workers.
He began to send copies of his letters not only to the Moscow
and Petrograd committees but also to district leaders. One
worker said,

> Not long ago we got a letter from Ilyich for delivery to the
> Central Committee. . . . We read the letter and gasped. It seems
> that Lenin had long ago put before the Central Committee the
> question of insurrection. We raised a row. We began to bring
> pressure on them.*

It was exactly what Lenin had had in mind.

Trotsky said, "At turning points in his policy, Lenin always
found somebody to rely on." When the Central Committee
turned a deaf ear, Lenin found Ivan T. Smilga, president of the
Regional Committee of the Soviets in Finland. On September
27 he wrote Smilga a very long letter.

> What are we doing? Only passing resolutions? We are losing
> time, we are setting "dates" (October 20—Congress of Soviets—

* *Ibid.,* 3:137.

Isn't it ridiculous to postpone this way? Isn't it ridiculous to rely on that?) The Bolsheviks are not carrying on a systematic work of preparing their armed forces for the overthrow of Kerensky. . . . We must agitate in the party for a serious attitude toward armed insurrection. . . . And further, as to your role. . . . To create a secret committee of the most loyal military men . . . collect (and yourself verify) the most accurate information about the make-up and position of the troops in and around Petrograd. . . .*

He outlined practical considerations such as troop movements. At this point, Lenin was obviously planning to attack from Finland, after having made sure of popular support within Petrograd.

Lenin had told the Bolsheviks that to time an insurrection for the opening of the congress was stupidity, that the government would anticipate such a move and would "get together the Cossacks for the day of that stupidly 'appointed' insurrection." He protested that successful insurrections are not advertised in advance, like a ballet performance. His frustration was such that he took a drastic step; he submitted his resignation to the Central Committee, saying that it had not responded to his pleas that the Bolsheviks seize power, that Bolshevik editors were printing his articles after intentional delays, and with the most biting criticisms edited out. "I feel compelled to request permission to withdraw from the Central Committee, which I hereby do, and leave myself freedom of agitation in the lower ranks of the party and at the party congress." His resignation was not acted on, and Lenin remained in the Central Committee, but he went on appealing directly to the workers, and they responded. At the end of September, the Moscow Regional Bureau accused the Central Committee of nonrevolutionary attitudes, and demanded that it take "a clear and definite course toward insurrection." The Central Committee, on October 3,

* *Ibid.*, 3:134.

decided "not to debate the question." But it was obviously feeling the pressures, and Lenin kept them up. Early in October he wrote, "The Bolsheviks have no right to await the Congress of Soviets. They ought to seize the power *right now.* . . . Delay is a crime."

At that moment, no one had power, and no one but Lenin seemed to want it. The Soviet was pleased to point out that the Provisional Government was merely facade; on September 25 it passed a resolution condemning the coalition as the government of the civil war, the bourgeois autocracy, and of counterrevolutionary violence. While the two governments wrangled, the country was being torn by peasant uprisings. The peasants numbered 90 percent of Russia's population; when they rioted, they shook the country. Now they were sick of waiting for the land to be given them, and they were taking it. In the process, they destroyed anything that would keep them from tilling it—cattle, manor houses, woodlots and orchards. Sukhanov wrote, "These were no longer 'excesses' as they had been in May and June. It was a mass phenomenon—tidal waves heaving and billowing throughout the country." Bolshevik influence was still not strong enough among the peasants so that the party could lead them. Insofar as they were anything, the peasants were usually Socialist Revolutionaries, and the SR party had no leadership to offer. So the peasants rampaged, and the Black Hundreds joined them in savage pogroms. The countryside was without government, anarchical, so troops were sent to suppress the disorders. There was repression—martial law and shooting of demonstrators. But the uprisings continued. Lenin had been courting the peasants by advocating immediate land seizure. Now the other parties were irate, not because he had stirred up the peasants—no one could claim to have started the riots except the peasants themselves, unless it was the governments which had promised them so much and given them nothing—but because Lenin had boldly adopted policies which the Socialist Revolutionaries and the anarchists had advocated for

15 years, and which he had always denounced. They ought not to have been surprised; Lenin had appropriated the Menshevik ideas of Soviets and the Military Revolutionary Committee in the same way.

But for Lenin, the land question was a tricky business. He wanted to gain peasant support, and to do that he demanded that the government give them land. But he hoped the government would not listen to his demands; he did not want the peasants to get the land until after they had helped the Bolsheviks into power through a revolution. If they got it before the Bolshevik coup they would go about their business and refuse to fight. And of course he did not want any other party to gain the credit for having given the peasants the land. But he had taken a chance and gone on haranguing, and the government had cooperated by doing nothing. Now Lenin could claim that the Bolsheviks were the "sole party fighting against the rich and the government for land, peace, and bread."

"Land, peace, and bread" summarized the nation's needs. If land was important to 90 percent of the population, bread was important to everyone. The cities were hungry, the countryside was hungry, and the soldiers at the front were literally starving. Morale was very low. As early as September 21, an officer who had come to speak to the Petrograd Soviet told them that the soldiers in the trenches weren't interested in talk of freedom or land now. "They want only one thing now—the end of the war. Whatever you may say here, the soldiers are not going to fight any more." So the issues were clear, if not simple: peace, bread, and land. The Provisional Government did nothing about any of these demands. The coming Constituent Assembly was the excuse now; all important decisions would be delayed until it could be elected. Then it would draft a constitution and set up a democratic government. Meanwhile, the Pre-Parliament would govern.

The Pre-Parliament was scheduled to meet on October 7 in the Marian Palace. Each party was planning to send its most prominent people; the Pre-Parliament might be powerless, but it promised to be brilliant. It opened at five o'clock in the afternoon, and the whole Bolshevik contingent arrived late. According to Sukhanov, the 66 Bolshevik delegates had held an eleventh-hour meeting to argue over whether or not they should attend, and were still emotional when they entered. According to Trotsky, there had been no such disagreement; the contingent had calmly voted on the fifth, and all but one member had opted to quit Pre-Parliament on opening day. They all knew how Lenin felt; he had written on September 23,

> We must boycott the Pre-Parliament. We must go out into the soviets . . . into the trade unions . . . in general to the masses. We must summon them to the struggle. We must give them a correct and clear slogan: To drive out the Bonapartist gang of Kerensky with its fake Pre-Parliament. . . . Long Live the boycott!*

In any case, by the time they reached the Marian Palace, the Bolsheviks were in agreement. When Trotsky took the floor, he castigated the Provisional Government, saying that its bourgeois members were plotting to prevent the Constituent Assembly. There was pandemonium as he went on to accuse it of treachery and "murderous intrigues against the people"; from the floor the bourgeois delegates loudly reviewed all the charges ever made against the Bolsheviks. Trotsky concluded that the Bolsheviks had "nothing whatever in common with this government of treason" and ended, "In withdrawing from the provisional council we summon the workers, soldiers, and peasants of all Russia to be on their guard. . . . Petrograd is in danger! The revolution is in danger! The people are in danger!" Then the Bolsheviks left in a body.

It would seem from this and from most Bolshevik writings of the period that the party was fighting desperately to protect

* Trotsky, *History of the Russian Revolution,* 2:340.

the embryo Constituent Assembly. In fact, the Bolshevik attitude was not simple, straightforward support. Lenin did not
want the assembly to meet until the Bolsheviks were already in
power, if then. But the idea of a Constituent Assembly had far
too much popular support for him to oppose it directly; instead, he was using it. Just as he had used the phrase "All
Power to the Soviet" instead of "All Power to the Bolsheviks,"
he now used the assembly as a smoke screen for the coup he
was planning. He represented the Constituent Assembly as
something in need of protection, and appeared to find enemies
of it everywhere. (Coincidentally, those enemies were always
enemies of the Bolsheviks as well.) Lenin took aim at the
Coalition Government; nearly every official Bolshevik statement
during this period contained the idea that the coalition was in
league with the bourgeoisie to undermine the Constituent Assembly. Bolshevik rank and file and the nonparty revolutionaries, who rallied to the defense, were warned that since the
coalition would try to subvert the assembly, the Soviet would
have to be ready to fight for the assembly's survival. Lenin
called the government "a gang of usurpers who had seized
autocratic power through private agreement among a couple of
dozen men," and at hundreds of mass meetings, workers and
soldiers protested this "shameful bourgeois plot" against the
revolution. Lenin moved subtly to try to shift distrust of the
government to distrust of the Constituent Assembly. Did anyone really think that such a government would allow an honest
Constituent Assembly?

The other political leaders knew that the Bolsheviks were
moving toward a showdown. Sukhanov wrote that when the
Bolsheviks flung aside their voting papers, that is, when they
left Pre-Parliament, they were in effect taking up their rifles.
He was right; action was imminent, and Lenin was coming to
Petrograd. The Central Committee had finally authorized his
return on October 3, and from the 7th on, he was "underground" in the workers' Vyborg District.

Отъ Военно-Революціоннаго Комитета при Петроградскомъ Совѣтѣ
Рабочихъ и Солдатскихъ Депутатовъ.

Къ Гражданамъ Россіи.

Временное Правительство низложено. Государственная власть перешла въ руки органа Петроградскаго Совѣта Рабочихъ и Солдатскихъ Депутатовъ Военно-Революціоннаго Комитета, стоящаго во главѣ Петроградскаго пролетаріата и гарнизона.

Дѣло, за которое боролся народъ: немедленное предложеніе демократическаго мира, отмѣна помѣщичьей собственности на землю, рабочій контроль надъ производствомъ, созданіе Совѣтскаго Правительства — это дѣло обезпечено.

ДА ЗДРАВСТВУЕТЪ РЕВОЛЮЦІЯ РАБОЧИХЪ, СОЛДАТЪ И КРЕСТЬЯНЪ!

Военно-Революціонный Комитетъ
при Петроградскомъ Совѣтѣ
Рабочихъ и Солдатскихъ Депутатовъ

25 октября 1917 г. 10 ч. утра.

A handbill proclamation, "From the Military Committee of the Petrograd Soviet of Workers' and Soldiers' Deputies."

To All the Citizens of Russia:

The Provisional Government is overthrown. The state power has passed into the hands of the organ of the Petrograd Soviet of Workers' and Soldiers' Deputies, and Military Revolutionary Committee, which stands at the head of the Petrograd proletariat and garrison.

The cause the people have been fighting for: the immediate proposal of a democratic peace, the abolition of landlord's property rights, workers' control of production and the creation of a Soviet Government—is achieved. Long live the revolution of workers, soldiers and peasants!

The Military Revolutionary Committee
of the Petrograd Soviet
of Workers' and Soldiers' Deputies.

October 20, 1917 10 a.m.

On October 9, the Petrograd Soviet voted to form a committee for defense, and the Military Revolutionary Committee was reactivated. (The Soviet's report of the Bolsheviks' withdrawal from the Pre-Parliament ended, "Long live the direct and open struggle for revolutionary power in the country.") On October 10, the Central Committee of the Bolshevik Party assembled for an important meeting. Nine of the 21 members were absent, but Lenin was there, still cleanshaven, bespectacled, and bewigged. (Ironically, they met in Menshevik Sukhanov's apartment. His wife was a staunch Bolshevik and had suggested that he save himself the long trip home that evening. Sukhanov later called it one of the "jokes of the merry muse of History.")

The committee had important business to transact, and the meeting lasted 10 hours, with tea, bread, and sausage served at intervals. All but two members agreed to rise as soon as possible, "depending on circumstances but not on the Congress," according to Trotsky.* Lenin enumerated the arguments against immediate action and refuted them all. The months of impatient waiting were over; he was in command, with Trotsky supporting him all the way. The committee adopted new agitational slogans to mirror the mood: "Further Delay is Impossible" and "It's Time to Pass from Words to Deeds."

The committee's resolution did not put an end to its disagreements. Instead, it brought them to public attention. On October 11, Zinoviev and Kamenev distributed a long objection to party members: "Before history, before the international proletariat, before the Russian revolution and the Russian working-class we have no right to stake the whole future . . . upon the card of armed insurrection. . . ." Their alternate plan was to participate in the Constituent Assembly as a strong opposition.

The government could hardly fail to notice what was afoot, and reacted in ways that helped the Bolsheviks. Kerensky tried to move troops that were known to be pro-Bolshevik to the front. This angered the soldiers and provoked their resistance. The Military Revolutionary Committee took advantage of their mood to create a Garrison Conference with the more important regiments, establishing one more line of communication. On October 13, the Petrograd Soldiers' Soviet voted to put all military power into the hands of the Military Revolutionary Committee. (Trotsky chaired the Military Revolutionary Committee—he was, in effect, the Bolshevik army's chief of staff.

---

* Reed wrote that Lenin timed the insurrection for the opening day of the Second All-Russian Congress of Soviets—October 23—in order to involve the provincial congressional delegates and give the movement an All-Russian quality, and that he cautioned against further delay because "it is difficult for a large organized body of people to take swift decisive action." Trotsky said Lenin wanted the insurrection to begin on or before the fifteenth—the congress was originally scheduled to open on the twentieth—but that difficulties of organization delayed it. While still in Finland, Lenin had repeatedly cautioned the Bolsheviks against beginning an insurrection on the opening day of the congress on the grounds that such a move would be anticipated.

The fact that he was also president of the Petrograd Soviet simplified Bolshevik problems.) The Bolsheviks had made sure that the Military Revolutionary Committee claimed representatives from every important group—all trade unions, the fleet, the army, and so forth—now each regiment had a commissar from the committee.

The government was concerned, but not greatly alarmed. Its members had seen signs of Bolshevik uprising for so long that they had come to take them for granted. Moreover, they knew there was serious dissension among the Bolsheviks; Zinoviev and Kamanev had not only leaked the plan of insurrection, but had published a long article against it on the seventeenth. Lenin wrote an even longer rebuttal, which ran from the nineteenth to the twenty-first. He wrote it not to convince Zinoviev and Kamanev, who, he proposed, should be dismissed from the party, but to influence readers who might have been led astray by them. His three-installment article implied armed uprising. Now at the last minute, the mavericks fell into line, the Bolsheviks closed ranks, and insurrection was on everyone's agenda.

10. Battle Plans

A review of strengths and weaknesses began. In the provinces, Soviet congresses were held everywhere, and showed great gains in Bolshevik power. On the fifteenth, the soldiers of Moscow had demonstrated: "We would rather die in Moscow on the barricades than go to the front." Obviously, the Bolsheviks had support from the Moscow garrison. At the front, the soldiers were interested in nothing but immediate peace, and although they were apolitical, would support the Bolsheviks because they were the only party promising peace. Agitators had been working for weeks, making sure that if any man would not fight for the Bolsheviks he would at least not fight against them.

The Bolsheviks had never been too busy with affairs of state to pay attention to the common people, which was one of their great strengths. Sukhanov wrote,

> . . . battlefront delegates not only . . . filed into Smolny and appeared in the big soviet meetings with their mandates and speeches. In addition, they persistently sought intimate chats and explicit, authoritative explanations from old soviet leaders. But these were not given to them. They were almost never received. When they were successful in catching a leader, they were sent away to a department of public information. Non-party or SR-minded delegates, disappointed and bitter, turned

at once to the Bolsheviks. At Smolny they poured out their souls to them and at the front became champions of their influence.*

Lenin thought it was important to reach and influence these men. He was counting on them to carry the Bolshevik message back to the villages when the war was over. If he couldn't influence the peasant directly, he might make contact through the returning veterans.

But the immediate problem was the rising in Petrograd, and by Lenin's timetable, it was running late. On the 17th, the All-Russian Soviet Central Executive Committee postponed the All-Russian Congress from October 20 to October 25. On the 18th, the Military Revolutionary Committee wired all army units to do nothing without its authorization. Leaders were invited to Smolny to hear the background to the order, and many came. The Soviet's Central Executive Committee declared the meeting incompetent, but it met anyway. It soon became apparent that the delegates had come to speak, rather than to listen, and they all said essentially the same thing. Izmailovskys, Chasseurs, Volhynians, Grenadiers, Cuxholms, Semyonovskys, Rifles, Pavlovskys, Electro-Technical Battalion, Moscow Regiment, the 89th—all said they would come out at the first call, and conveyed mistrust of the government, sometimes of the Central Executive Committee as well. Of those present, only the cavalry maintained neutrality. (The cavalry, recruited from well-to-do peasants, said "All Power to the Soviet.")

On October 19, the Central Executive Committee called a meeting with the regimental and company committees of all units. The delegates repeated the sentiments of the previous evening. Finally, on Saturday, October 21, there was a meeting of the regimental and company committees at which three decisions were made: one, the garrison promised to put all its resources at the disposal of the Soviet congress, and to help it take power in order to secure land, peace, and bread; two,

* Sukhanov, *Zapiski o Revoliutsii,* 7:70.

the garrison promised full support to the Military Revolutionary Committee; three, on the next day, the twenty-second, the garrison would be on the alert in case the bourgeoisie tried to "create a counterrevolutionary atmosphere" during the peaceful muster of forces which was scheduled. In effect, the garrison acknowledged the Soviet as the sole government and the Military Revolutionary Committee as its army officers and police force, and promised to support the whole structure.

After the garrison meeting, members of the Military Revolutionary Committee went to see District Commander Polkovnikov with word that henceforth all orders to the garrison would have to be countersigned by their representative. He refused to acknowledge their authority. The delegates reported back to Trotsky, who called an emergency meeting of the Soviet for the 23rd.

Meanwhile, the Soviet had designated Sunday, October 22, as a day for "peaceful review of forces" in Petrograd. The turnout was tremendous. Trotsky and others addressed meetings attended by thousands of enthusiastic workers. Sukhanov wrote, "There was a mood very near to ecstasy." The people needed a morale-booster; not only were food, clothing, and fuel uncomfortably scarce, but September and October are Petrograd's rainy season, with bleak, dark, windy days. Reed wrote that it got dark at about three in the afternoon and didn't really lighten again until about ten the next morning. The city was a sea of mud, and few workers had enough clothes to stay dry.

On the same day as the "peaceful review," there was an all-city conference of Red Guards, with 100 delegates representing about 20,000 fighters. Trotsky noted that the figures weren't to be taken too seriously, since not all those registered had shown signs of real involvement. The coup was already beginning, but these forces still thought of themselves as defenders, rather than aggressors. And the government still thought it had the upper hand. Many felt that Kerensky actually wanted the

Bolsheviks to attempt a coup so that he could destroy the party once and for all.

On October 23, Smolny buzzed with last-minute activity. Sukhanov noted a new look there, a new crowd of gray, faceless men. "Everything was dirty and messy and reeked of cheap tobacco, boots, and damp overcoats." There were armed soldiers and sailors everywhere. But Smolny, which still housed the Soviet as well as the Bolshevik party, was still open to all, and no more fortified than before.

The emergency meeting of the Soviet called by Trotsky was now in session, dealing with two related problems: the army general staff's refusal to recognize the Military Revolutionary Committee and the fact that the commandant of Peter-Paul had refused to recognize the commissar whom the committee had sent there—in fact had threatened to arrest him. The Bolsheviks assumed that if the Soviet was not allowed its (Bolshevik) representative at Peter-Paul, then the fortress must be considered a government stronghold. They couldn't allow the government to hole up there; Peter-Paul had an arsenal of 100,000 rifles and was by definition a fortress. (Its outer wall was 60 feet thick.) It would have to be taken and occupied before any insurrection could succeed. One member proposed that they attack immediately with a battalion of the Pavlovsky, but the general feeling was that this was both futile and risky—the place was much easier to hold than to take, and in any case, such an act could scarcely have been ignored, even by a government as blind as the coalition. Instead, Trotsky proposed that he go to Peter-Paul and talk the garrison into supporting the Bolsheviks. What did they have to lose?

A message went out to all units of the garrison explaining that on October 21 the Petrograd garrison had agreed to consider the Military Revolutionary Committee its governing body, but that now the army's general staff refused to recognize or work with the committee. By refusing to honor the garrison's decision, the staff had shown itself to be counterrevolutionary, the message said. Then it called on the soldiers to combat such threats to the revolution by refusing to follow orders unless they were signed by the Military Revolutionary Committee. At Peter-Paul, the garrison welcomed Trotsky enthusiastically, listened closely, and almost unanimously passed a resolution to rise against the bourgeois government in defense of the Soviet. They installed the commissar under their protection, and refused to recognize the commandant. The Bolsheviks gained 100,000 rifles, not to mention the building and the men.

District Commander Polkovnikov, of the government's forces, had also scheduled a staff meeting on the 23rd, with representatives of the Central Executive Committee and the regimental committees invited. The Bolsheviks stayed just long enough to repeat their views. The staff kept reassuring the government that the whole thing was simply a misunderstanding brought about because a commissar had not been confirmed, and that it would soon be set straight. Meanwhile, the Military Revolutionary Committee was issuing orders over the staff's head, the soldiers were refusing to act on orders not signed by the Military Revolutionary Committee, and in effect, the general staff had been cut out of the administration of the army.

That night, the 23rd, the garrison representatives met at Smolny; they were invited to a session of the Soviet which opened at 7:00 P.M. It was very crowded. Sukhanov remembered that he was struck by the absurdity of the situation when the Military Revolutionary Committee made its report. "The chief of staff of the rebel troops was making a resounding report on all the measures and tactical steps of his staff—heard not only by his own army, but also by the enemy army and its staff." Of course the Military Revolutionary Committee thought of itself as a Soviet, rather than a purely Bolshevik, organization. No one had told the general membership anything else! Its report said that the committee had established effective censorship of all "suspect" printing orders; placed commissars in all the garrison units and made sure that no orders were obeyed which had not been approved by these commissars; put a commissar in the Peter-Paul, and been given access to its arsenal; and was stockpiling arms in all the factory stores, to be distributed to workers at the order of the Military Revolutionary Committee. Vladimir Alexandrovich Antonov made the report; he was asked if he knew that Kerensky had ordered troops to Petrograd from the front. Antonov said cheerfully that the committee knew all about it, and that most of the troops would refuse to come. There were only a few military cadet detachments that he was unsure of, and if these attempted to come to Kerensky's aid they would be stopped on the way.

The Mensheviks and SRs could hardly help but notice that this was insurrection. Trotsky answered that yes, "an insurrection is going on, and the Bolsheviks, in the form of the congress majority, will take the power into their own hands. The steps taken by the Military Revolutionary Committee are steps for the seizure of power. . . ." It could hardly have been plainer. The report of the Military Revolutionary Committee was approved, and the committee was charged with taking precautions against riots, looting, and other acts of lawlessness. The next day it issued an order in no uncertain terms: "At the first attempt of criminal elements to bring about disturbances, looting, knifing, or shooting on the streets of Petrograd, the criminals will be wiped off the face of the earth."

While Smolny worked, the general staff met. Kerensky spent the night of October 23 facing the reality of the situation: Peter-Paul had been occupied, and demands that the commissars be removed had been refused. He had already called up all reliable units. The general staff now could think of nothing better to do than to write a great sheaf of orders, everything from outlawing the Military Revolutionary Committee to ordering car-owners to turn their cars over to the government to prevent their being seized by Bolsheviks. (No one did. Sukhanov noted that during the next day the government lost even its own cars.) All the orders were hardly worth the paper they were written on; there was no force to back them up.

In the very early morning of the twenty-fourth, the general

staff sent forces to the Bolshevik printing plant to shut it down.
(Sukhanov bewails the fact that they didn't move against
Smolny with a scratch detachment. Attacking the printing plant
was just as "counterrevolutionary," and was futile; the Bolsheviks had already demonstrated their ability to resurrect their
publications. And Smolny was still unfortified; it might have
been taken at that point.) But Bolshevik strength grew hourly.
At 5:30 that morning two torpedo boats from Helsingfors came
up the Neva. The Baltic Fleet hadn't waited to be called; the
sailors had sent themselves with "Greetings for the Congress."
The Second All-Russian Congress of Soviets was scheduled to
open on October 25.

Meanwhile, the Military Revolutionary Committee had
learned of the destruction of the Bolsheviks' newspaper. Two
workers had run panting to Smolny, saying that if the committee
would give them a guard, they'd bring out the paper. No sooner
said than done; members of the Litovsky Regiment and the
Sixth Battalion of sappers tore the seals from the building and
the paper came out only a few hours late. The government's
action pleased the Bolsheviks; Trotsky said,

> . . . these pinpricks were just sufficient to convict the government
> of preparing a counter-revolutionary *coup d'etat*. Although an
> insurrection can win only on the offensive, it develops better
> the more it looks like self-defense. A piece of official sealing-wax
> on the door of the Bolshevik editorial rooms—as a military
> measure that is not much. But what a superb signal for battle!*

It was all they needed. Telegrams were sent to all garrisons:
"The enemy of the people took the offensive during the night.
The Military Revolutionary Committee is leading the resist-
ance. . . ."

The Bolsheviks had begun to fortify Smolny during the
night. By the time they finished, it was an armed camp. By

---

* Trotsky, *History of the Russian Revolution*, 3:207–208.

that afternoon there were 200–300 provincial delegates in Petrograd for the coming Soviet Congress, and the Bolsheviks immediately gave them a place in the insurrection. (They were not given the whole background, however. Trotsky noted, "Whatever is said at a large meeting inevitably gets abroad.") At two in the afternoon, a deputation arrived from the Petrograd Duma. It was sent away dissatisfied, but the fact that it had come illustrated the government's helplessness.

The Bolsheviks needed all available forces, and thought the Bicycle Battalion at Peter-Paul had been ominously evasive. Like the cavalry, bicyclists were recruited from the wealthy peasants, and were better educated and more self-confident than common soldiers. Trotsky, himself the son of a wealthy peasant, said that if a man found himself atop "two wheels with a chain—at least in a poor country like Russia—" his vanity would begin to swell like his tires. He added that in America it took a car to produce the same effect. But he wasted no time in getting to them, and won them over. After they declared allegiance to the Military Revolutionary Committee, they refused to go on guarding the Winter Palace, meeting place of the government. They had to be replaced with junkers,* thus further depleting the very small body of defenders at the government's command.

The government had tried to rally its forces, but most measures open to it were futile by now. It had ordered the junkers to stand prepared, and the *Aurora* to join the fleet at sea. (Everyone knew she was committed to the revolution.) It ordered the bridges over the Neva raised, and cut Smolny off the telephone system.

Being without telephone service inconvenienced Smolny, but

* This is another example of confusing Russian terminology. "Junkers" were young, usually upper-class men from the officers' candidate schools, a group which in the West might be called cadets. The transliteration "kadets," sometimes spelled "cadets," refers to members of the Constitutional Democratic party, and has nothing to do with the military.

the other measures were useless. The raising of the bridges, aside from signaling the population that an insurrection had begun, merely gave the opposing forces exercise. All day long they argued over the bridges, raising or lowering them depending on who had superior strength at that moment. The *Aurora*, when she received orders to put to sea, asked Smolny what to do. Smolny told her to stay, and to protect herself with "tugs, steam-boats, and cutters." She was now the Bolsheviks' primary means of communication—her radio was broadcasting Bolshevik instructions to the garrisons.

Meanwhile, in the early afternoon of the 24th, Kerensky dashed into a session of Pre-Parliament and made a long speech, saying, "Calls for insurrection appear daily in Bolshevik papers," and quoting Lenin at length to prove it. He also read a copy of a telegram from the Military Revolutionary Committee instructing the garrison to "make the regiment ready for battle and await further orders," adding, "in the language of the law and of judicial authority that is called a state of insurrection." Miliukov said that "Kerensky pronounced these words in the complacent tone of a lawyer who has at last succeeded in getting evidence against his opponent." Kerensky concluded that those groups which had dared to defy the state were "liable to immediate, decisive, and permanent liquidation." Tremendous applause, except from the Internationalists. Then he asked, "Can the government fulfill its duty with confidence in the support of this lofty assemblage?" It was a request for a vote of confidence, and Pre-Parliament recessed to let the factions consult.

That evening, Pre-Parliament reopened. Its reply to Kerensky was so hedged about with modifiers and clauses that it constituted a vote of no-confidence; moreover, the left-wing SRs had bolted to the Bolsheviks. Kerensky was stunned and tried to resign, but his colleagues assured him that he was overreacting to a problem which was really semantical and superficial, and that they had complete trust in him. He did not resign, but there was little he could do now except to respond to attack. The Bolsheviks sent a detachment of sailors led by a commissar to occupy the government telegraph agency and began censoring wires to the provinces. Kerensky sent an armored car manned by junkers; the sailors surrendered without a struggle. (If the Pre-Parliament had been united, the Bolsheviks might still have won, but it would have been much harder for them.)

The next day Kerensky borrowed a car from the American embassy and went to meet the troops coming from the front. Trotsky said, "Things were going badly with the regime, if the head of the government had to fly off with an American flag at his back to meet a bicycle brigade." Worse still, the brigade wasn't coming. It had joined the Bolsheviks. The insurrection was building, and the government's clumsy attempts to combat it didn't even slow it down.*

At 10:45 P.M. Lenin, still in disguise, arrived at Smolny. It was a scene of controlled confusion, with hundreds of workers coming and going. The unheated rooms reeked of wet, unwashed clothes and stale smoke. Lenin was more calm than most men would have been in the situation—his dream was about to be enacted. In fact, the first act had begun, and not even the playwright knew how it would end. But Lenin was confident that the time was ripe. Before coming to Smolny he had written,

. . . it is now absolutely clear that to delay the uprising would be fatal.

With all my might I urge comrades to realize that everything

---

* Most of these attempts appear to have been the result of an individual undertaking, not of an overall plan. For example, an army colonel took about a dozen junkers into the Vyborg District to try to arrest Lenin—the government had decided to rearrest all Bolsheviks out on bail, as well. The colonel had, for reasons best known to himself, decided that Lenin would be in the Bolshevik editorial office. (Lenin wasn't.) But the colonel couldn't find the office, and instead accidently entered a workers' club. The workers informed the Red Guard, who arrested the group and took them to Peter-Paul.

now hangs by a thread, that we are confronted by problems
which are not to be solved by conferences or congresses . . . but
exclusively by peoples, by the masses, by the struggle of armed
people. . . . We must at all costs, this very evening, this very
night, arrest the government. . . . We must not wait! We may
lose everything!*

The ubiquitous Sukhanov was at Smolny that night; he had
gone to observe a joint session of the worker-soldier and
peasant central executive committees scheduled for 11:00 P.M.
(Passes were demanded, but "a determined look and the statement, 'Member of the Central Executive Committee,' " got him
inside.) He was surprised at the size of the crowd; the ordinary
workers were now inside Smolny. Gray faces above gray coats.
"The mood too was gray. Faces were tired, dull, even gloomy.
There was no enthusiasm." There was no energy; the workers
were chronically undernourished, and lately they had been
sleeping when and where they dropped from exhaustion, often
on the wet floors of Smolny.

Nothing new was said in public that night, but outside the
Bolshevik army had begun its offensive. It was a motley army:
the Red Guard, armed workers, were its oldest members. Some
had retained the guns issued by the Provisional Government
during the Kornilov Rebellion, others had been more recently
armed.† Then there were Petrograd's soldiers. Trotsky did not
overestimate these men. He said that the typical regiments

---

* Lenin, *Collected Works,* 26:234.

† Trotsky recalled how, when the first workers came asking for arms,
he had told them, "But the arsenals are not in our hands." The workmen
had told him that the Sestroretsk Arms Factory would deliver if the
Soviet ordered. . . . What a convenient coincidence that Trotsky was
both president of the Petrograd Soviet and chairman of the Military
Revolutionary Committee! His first order for 5,000 rifles was filled the
same day. And when Peter-Paul came over to the Bolsheviks, its arsenal
supplied a constant line of delegates from the factories; the Factory and
Shop Committee room at Smolny was crowded with men waiting for
orders for rifles.

were disorganized and could not have sustained prolonged combat, but that at least they had had some experience under fire. All the units were united by a single sentiment, "Overthrow Kerensky as soon as possible, disperse, and go home and institute a new land system." There were also the sailors. At midnight, the Military Revolutionary Committee sent a coded telegram to the chairman of the Central Baltic Fleet: "Send regulations." According to Trotsky, "regulations" translated, "1,500 chosen Baltic sailors armed to the teeth." He relied on the sailors; not only were they of worker, rather than peasant, background, but they were coming from active duty. (Some of the army reserves were very rusty.)

And if the Bolshevik military forces were uncertain, the bourgeoisie's were nonexistent. The government had thought it could depend on the military elite—officers, junkers, shock battalions, and probably the Cossacks. These did not match the Bolshevik forces in numbers, but they were far better trained and disciplined. At the last minute, though, the Cossacks declared that they would not fight unless the infantry supported them; they said it would be suicidal. The Cossacks were tired of being thought of as machines to fight other people's battles. They wanted to go home too. The junkers at the Pavlovsky Academy also refused to fight; they feared instant reprisal from their neighbors, the Grenadier Regiment, which was pro-Bolshevik. In the end the government had only a few officers and junkers, and a totally untried women's force called more melodramatically than logically, the Death Battalion. Not even the most optimistic could believe that it would be enough.

11. The Bolshevik Offensive, October 25

The Bolshevik's main operation began at 2.00 A.M. on October 25. Originally, their plan had depended on a combination of Baltic sailors and armed workers. The sailors were to have come into Finland Station, which the Bolsheviks already held; there they were to have met the Vyborg district workers and Red Guards, and moved out from this stronghold of worker power, consolidating their gains as they went. Trotsky said that they had made this plan on the assumption that the government would fight back, but that events made them revise their strategy. "It was unnecessary to start from a limited base, because the government proved open to attack wherever the insurrectionists found it necessary to strike a blow."

Instead of the original plan, small parties occupied railroad stations, power plants, the main bridges, the waterworks, the telephone and telegraph offices—they cut off the Winter Palace, thus revenging themselves for Smolny's cutoff—then moved on to the big printing houses, and finally, the State Bank. They left guards behind in each place. The whole thing was done without bloodshed. Sukhanov said that the Bolshevik takeover resembled a changing of the guard—the government forces surrendered to the Bolsheviks without a shot having been fired, and as one group walked in, the other walked out. Trotsky said that everyone involved in the insurrection had "absolute confidence that victory was going to be won without casualties."

Sukhanov played armchair general at some length. This was not his war; he had no sympathy with either side. He couldn't understand why the Bolsheviks had not tried to take the Winter Palace during the first night, since leaving the government in session was dangerous—it might have led to full-scale civil war. But no attempt was made to occupy the palace, although one minister was arrested. The joint executive committee session of the Soviet ended at 4:00 A.M. on the 25th. By then, Trotsky had made it plain; it was insurrection, and the Bolsheviks were winning with no contest.

In the morning, General Levitsky wired General Kukhonin from the War Ministry, which the Bolsheviks had not yet taken, that the Petrograd garrison had joined the Bolsheviks, that the town was full of sentries, that the troops in the Winter Palace had decided not to come out actively. "The Provisional Government finds itself in the capital of a hostile state which has finished mobilization but not yet begun active operations."

At 10:00 A.M., the Military Revolutionary Committee sent out a proclamation:

> To All the Citizens of Russia:
>
> The Provisional Government is overthrown. The state power has passed into the hands of the organ of the Petrograd Soviet of Workers' and Soldiers' Deputies, the Military Revolutionary Committee, which stands at the head of the Petrograd proletariat and garrison.
>
> The cause the people have been fighting for: the immediate proposal of a democratic peace, the abolition of landlords' property rights, workers' control of production, and the creation of a Soviet Government—is achieved. Long live the revolution of workers, soldiers, and peasants!

The same message was radioed all over the country. It probably seemed to those who heard it in the provinces that a great change had taken place in Petrograd. Actually, the physical facts of life there were just as they had been for weeks—the Bolsheviks still held the real power, and the government still sat in the Winter Palace.

Considering the weariness and depression of the people, it was a very orderly uprising. The upper classes were more annoyed than fearful. Most were sure that the troops from the front would soon set things right. Meanwhile, they were not afraid to speak their minds to the Bolshevik soldiers who patrolled the streets, and the soldiers were somewhat sheepish and apologetic. Sukhanov went to the Marian Palace and found 15 to 20 workers and sailors in possession. They told him genially that they had just ousted the Pre-Parliament. He wrote,

> No one was in the Palace anymore, and they wouldn't let me in. But they didn't arrest me. No, they didn't want me. Members of the Central Executive Committee, generally speaking, were not touched. And by the way, did I know where the Provisional Government was? They had looked for it in the Marian Palace but had not found it. They would have arrested the ministers but they didn't know where they were. But just let them catch Kerensky or somebody. However, the conversation was quite amiable.*

From the Marian Palace, Sukhanov headed for Smolny, arriving at about 3:00 P.M. He had no trouble getting in, and went straight to the great hall, where an emergency session of the Petrograd Soviet was in progress. Trotsky had opened it, saying:

> In the name of the Military Revolutionary Committee I declare that the Provisional Government no longer exists. . . . The revolutionary garrison has dismissed the meeting of the Pre-Parliament. People said that the insurrection would set off a pogrom and deluge the revolution in a torrent of blood. For

* Sukhanov, *Zapiski o Revoliutsii,* 7:71.

now, all that has taken place is bloodless. We do not know of one victim. I do not know of an example in history of a revolutionary movement which involved such masses and which took place so bloodlessly. The Winter Palace has still not been taken, but its fate will be decided in the course of the next few minutes.*

Sukhanov had arrived late. When he entered the hall, "an unfamiliar, bald-headed, and clean-shaven man stood speaking heatedly on the platform. But he spoke in a strangely familiar, hoarse, loud voice with guttural inflections and very distinctive accents at the ends of phrases. Ah! Lenin!" After 111 days underground, Lenin was showing himself, at least in the relative safety of Smolny. Trotsky had presented him and he had been welcomed with tumultuous applause. Sukhanov missed much of his speech, due to his late arrival, the noise in the hall, and the distractions—the place was crowded with workers. But he heard Lenin say that the masses would shape the new government in the form of Soviet organizations, and that this third Russian Revolution must finally lead to the victory of socialism. Lenin went on to speak of ending the war and redistributing the land.

The Soviet had a problem: its SR, Menshevik, and Independent delegates didn't want to be associated with this insurrection, and weren't quite sure what to do about it. At the opening of the session, there had been 650 voting delegates present; about 390 of them were Bolsheviks. Toward the end of the session, there were about 900 delegates present. During the recess, the factions caucused, and an SR resolution to withdraw was defeated 92 to 60. By evening, right and left SRs were meeting in separate rooms. At eight o'clock the Mensheviks asked for a longer recess, because they had "too many opinions."

Across town, where Trotsky had said that the fate of the Winter Palace would be decided in "a few minutes," there was

* *Ibid.*, pp. 174–175.

equal indecision within and without. Inside, the ministers could do little except hope that Kerensky would arrive with troops in time to save them. Many believed that if the Bolsheviks occupied the palace, they would kill as they came, and that if they did not occupy it, they would demolish it. (The Winter Palace is across the Neva River from Peter-Paul, and a fine target either for the fortress' big guns or for any warship on the river.) Now Bolshevik forces surrounded it, cruisers, gunboats, and minelayers were within range. And the palace's vast size—it contains more than 1,000 rooms—made it vulnerable to sneak attack; the 2,000 or so men and women defending it were lost in its corridors and halls.

But the revolutionaries were undecided too. It took them hours to agree on strategy; they finally reached a decision, and then ran into physical problems. They needed a red lantern to signal the beginning of the attack. No one had a red lantern. And when they finally found one, they couldn't tie it to a pole in the right position. The artillery men were becoming irritable about what the rain would do to their cherished guns, and wanted to get on with things. Finally, at 9:45 P.M. the cruiser *Aurora* fired a blank from her six-inch cannon to signal the opening of attack, and Peter-Paul began shelling. (Most of the shells, by accident or design, passed overhead. Very little damage was done.)

John Reed and three companions, one a woman, had walked into the Winter Palace that afternoon by showing American passports and saying, "Official business!" to the sentries. Inside, "the place was all a huge barrack, and evidently had been for weeks from the look of the floor and walls. Machine guns were mounted on window sills, rifles stacked between the mattresses." They wandered through the building, conversing with anyone who seemed to want to talk; no one seemed surprised at their presence.

By evening, the defenders inside the palace were having second thoughts. Many of the junkers had left their weapons in the entrance and gone home, in obedience to orders received from the commandant of the Konstantinovsky School, who had been talked into giving the order by the Military Revolutionary Committee. Most of the government's artillerymen had left, taking with them four of the defenders' six guns. The Pavlovsky Regiment arrested them as they left, took the guns, and set up two. The Women's Death Battalion was gone too. According to Trotsky, many had been arrested during their misguided attempt to free General Alekseiev, who had been taken prisoner by the clerks at General Headquarters. But according to Sukhanov, they had simply gone home. "They had felt like it and left, like the Cossacks. It was clear that the besiegers were letting hostile detachments through like water through a sieve." The sieve leaked in both directions; the Bolsheviks had been trickling into the palace for some time. There were skirmishes here and there, but no one was badly hurt. Some of the officers had got affably drunk on the palace's wine and were fencing with each other for the fun of it.

During the evening, Reed and his group wandered among the besiegers outside the palace. He said,

> Here the street cars had stopped running, but a few blocks away we could see the trams, the crowds, the lighted shop windows, and the electric signs of the moving picture shows—life going on as usual. We had tickets to the Ballet at the Marinsky Theatre —all the theatres were open—but it was too exciting out of doors. . . .
>
> Up the Nevsky [the main street of Petrograd] the whole city seemed to be out promenading. On every corner immense crowds were massed around a core of hot discussion. Pickets of a dozen soldiers with fixed bayonets lounged at the street-crossings, red-faced old men in rich fur coats shook their fists at them, and smartly dressed women screamed epithets; the soldiers argued feebly, with embarrassed grins.*

Trotsky wrote, "To the respectable and educated strata of the capital it was of no consequence apparently that their govern-

* Reed, *Ten Days that Shook the World,* p. 83.

ment was under fire.... Chaliapin had been incomparable in
Don Carlos."

Eleven o'clock came, and at Smolny the Congress was still in
session. Everyone knew about the insurrection, but no one
seemed to care. Sukhanov attributed the grayness of the emotional atmosphere to the type of audience. He saw these
rank-and-file revolutionaries as "utterly crude and ignorant,"
motivated by wholly subjective emotions and needs—malice, des-
pair, hunger—rather than by understanding of socialism or any
other abstract theory. Reed was there too; he said that an
anarchist delegate made room for him. "Unshaven and filthy, he
was reeling from three nights of sleepless work on the Military
Revolutionary Committee." The anarchist was typical of the
crowd, revolutionaries who had little in common except the
need to take some action to better their conditions. They were
gray men in gray coats—soldiers' overcoats; civilian clothing
was almost impossible for a poor man to buy. And Sukhanov
himself had explained their lack of enthusiasm, in another con-
text. When he went home to dinner that night, he realized that
in earlier days he'd not have dreamed of leaving the scene of
action. He said that everyone had been so bludgeoned by recent events that their senses were blunted, and nothing could
arouse them any more. But he was right in thinking of the
majority as apolitical; the average peasant-soldier could not
have outlined the background or platform of the Bolshevik
party. And during the evening, the Menshevik Martov, a long-
time opponent of Lenin's policies, said:

> We must put a stop to military action on both sides. . . . The
> question of power is beginning to be decided by conspiratorial
> methods. . . . A civil war threatens us with an explosive of
> counter-revolution, a peaceful solution of the crisis can be
> achieved only by creating a government which will be recognized
> by the whole democracy.*

* Trotsky, *History of the Russian Revolution,* 3:307.

There was tremendous applause from the very forces which were making the insurrection.

But it was too late for anyone to pull the Bolsheviks back, even though the president of the Executive Committee of the Peasants' Soviet summoned the peasants to abandon this "untimely" congress and go to the Winter Palace "to die with those who were sent there to do our will." A sailor from the *Aurora* told him that they were only firing blanks at the palace, adding, "Proceed with your business in peace."

Lenin waited in another room at Smolny. There was no furniture in the room, but someone had put rugs and pillows on the floor. He and Trotsky "took a rest there lying side by side." But Trotsky kept being called out, and a steady procession of people came in to tell them what was going on in the assembly hall and outside.

Across town, the Duma members (except for its Bolshevik faction) had decided to march to the Winter Palace in order to die with the government, and the peasants' deputies from the congress had joined them. (Everyone but the Bolsheviks seems to have been determined to die heroically in the Bolshevik revolution.) Three to four hundred men set out through the rainy dark, carrying umbrellas and lanterns. They sang the "Marseillaise" and tramped bravely enough till they reached the Ekaterina Canal, where a patrol of armed sailors told them, "Go home and leave us alone." The Duma stood around for a while, but it was one thing to die heroically and another to stand out in the rain. They "got chilly and decided to go back," wrote Stankevich, who was one of the marchers.

Inside the Winter Palace, the government officials were trying to meet their fates with dignity, but were uncertain of their roles in this drama. One member later said,

> We wandered through the gigantic mousetrap, meeting occasionally, either all together or in small groups, for brief conversations —condemned people, lonely, abandoned by all. . . . Around us

vacancy, within us vacancy, and in this grew up the soulless
courage of placid indifference.*

Rumors still managed to penetrate the palace. Trotsky wrote
that word that the Duma was coming "with the people" was
joyfully received. Supposedly, "The public men, the merchantry,
the people with clergy at their head . . . [were] marching this
way to free the beleaguered palace." Later, hundreds of Bolsheviks were allowed in through the main door in the mistaken belief that they were the deputation from the Duma.

The palace never did surrender; slowly the defenders leaked
out and the besiegers trickled in. At last, when there were almost as many attackers as defenders inside, the "Duma delegation" broke in through the front door. The junkers who were
still loyal asked the ministers if they should fight to the death,
but the ministers said no, there was no need for bloodshed. The
Bolsheviks agreed. According to Trotsky, they were "armed to
the teeth. Lifted hands hold revolvers. Hand grenades hang
from belts. But nobody shoots and nobody throws a grenade."
The Bolsheviks poured in through the long corridors; in their
meeting room, the ministers sat round a table as though in session. The revolutionaries arrested them without incident and
packed them off to Truebetskoy Bastion, but the next day they
were transferred to house arrest. The Bolsheviks did not arrest
anyone but the government's officials. Not only were palace
servants allowed to go, but also the defending soldiers, with the
understanding that they would take no further action against the
Military Revolutionary Committee. When looting (by both
sides) began, the Red Guards stopped it, and searched everyone as he left the building. "Comrades . . . that is the property
of the people."

At Smolny, the Congress of Soviets had recessed at about
2:00 A.M., October 26. When it resumed, the delegates were
told that the Winter Palace had capitulated, and that the

* *Ibid.,* 3:261.

whole government, except for Kerensky, had been arrested. The revolution was accomplished; there was "no other power in Russia but the power of the Soviets," said Trotsky. When Lenin heard the news, he said, "The transition from the state of illegality, being driven in every direction, to power—is too rough." He added in German, "It makes one dizzy." Then, though he had professed atheism since the age of 16, he made the sign of the cross. Lenin was a complicated man.

But the congress was not made dizzy by the news; it hardly seemed to grasp its implications. One declaration followed another until at 5:17 A.M. Nikolai Vasilyevich Krylenko, who was to be commander in chief of the armies after the insurrection, "staggeringly tired," came in with a telegram: the Twelfth Army sent greetings and said it had formed a Military Revolutionary Committee which was guarding the northern front, and that the government's generals had been removed from command, and that all echelons ordered to move against the insurrection had come over to the Military Revolutionary Committee. At last the Bolsheviks dared believe they had been successful. Reed said there was "pandemonium . . . men weeping, embracing each other." The enthusiasm which had seemed nonexistent at the beginning of the session swept the ranks.

Then Lunacharsky read the Bolshevik proclamation, which had now become the new government's program. It proposed immediate peace, transfers of land to the peasants, democratization of the army, and nationalization of production. It also promised to summon the Constituent Assembly and to guarantee the rights of the nations of Russia to self-determination. Twelve delegates abstained from voting, but everyone else was in favor. Trotsky wrote, "The delegates had hardly strength left to applaud." The session ended at about 6:00 A.M. in a cold gray dawn.

12. A New Beginning, October 26

Petrograd had a new government, but the upper class still didn't know it. The bourgeois newspapers printed articles written before the decisive developments, and still forecast the arrival of troops from the front to put the Bolsheviks in their place. They advocated a boycott of the Bolsheviks, and sabotage of Bolshevik efforts. Many cooperated. There was brief mention that the Winter Palace had been seized, but as if it were a condition that would soon be changed.

But anyone who saw Smolny knew that it was now the seat of a government. Trotsky wrote that in Russia then, the automobile was more a sign of sovereignty than were the orb and scepter. Until that day, the automobiles had been apportioned among the government, the Central Executive Committee, and private owners. Now all were confiscated and taken to Smolny, which looked like a huge military garage. The Military Revolutionary Committee were still hard at work there, receiving delegates, informants, and couriers, sending out orders and commissars. The workers were exhausted and filthy from days and nights of work without a break, "and if they did not fall half dead on the floor, it seemed only thanks to the surrounding chaos which whirled them about and carried them away again. . . ." Trotsky wrote:

> Never since the creation of the world have so many orders been issued—by word of mouth, by pencil, by typewriter, by wire . . . thousands and myriads of orders, not always issued by those having the right, and rarely to those capable of carrying them out. But just there lay the miracle—that in this crazy whirlpool there turned out to be an inner meaning. People managed to understand each other. The most important things got done. Replacing the old web of administration, the first threads of the new were strung. The revolution grew in strength.*

During that day, October 26, the Central Committee of the Bolsheviks tried to start the wheels of the new government turning, and made its most important appointments. Lenin was named premier. (His official title was chairman of the Council of the People's Commissars; the Bolsheviks had decided that "ministers" sounded too bourgeois.) Trotsky was appointed people's commissar for foreign affairs, and others were given the portfolios of popular education, finance, labor, agriculture, nationalities, interior, industry and commerce, justice, supply, and posts and telegraphs. A board was appointed to military and naval affairs.

That evening the congress reopened. There were only three subjects on the agenda, but they were fundamental: peace, land, and government. Lenin, who had not yet addressed the congress, took the floor, receiving an overwhelming ovation. Reed, an ardent admirer, wrote:

> It was just 8:40 when a thundering wave of cheers announced the entrance of the presidium with Lenin—great Lenin—among them. A short, stocky figure, with a big head set down in his shoulders, bald and bulging. Little eyes, a snubbish nose, wide generous mouth and heavy chin; clean-shaven now but already beginning to bristle with the well-known beard. . . . Dressed in shabby clothes, his trousers much too long for him. Unimpressive to be the idol of a mob, loved and revered as perhaps few

* *Ibid.,* 3:322.

The New York Times.

THE WEATHER

Fair today and tomorrow; moderate northwest to north winds.

"All the News That's Fit to Print."

NEW YORK, FRIDAY, NOVEMBER 9, 1917.—TWENTY-TWO PAGES.

VOL. ... NO. 21,839.

REVOLUTIONISTS SEIZE PETROGRAD; KERENSKY FLEES; PLEDGE IS GIVEN TO SEEK "AN IMMEDIATE PEACE"; ITALIANS AGAIN DRIVEN BACK; LOSE 17,000 MORE MEN.

MINISTERS UNDER ARREST

Winter Palace Is Taken After Fierce Defense by Women Soldiers.

FORT'S GUNS TURNED ON IT

Cruiser and Armored Cars Also Brought Into Battle Waged by Searchlight.

TROTZKY HEADS REVOLT

Giving Land to the Peasants and Calling of Constituent Assembly Promised.

AWAITS LIGHT FROM RUSSIA

Washington Reserves Judgment, Hoping Revolt Is Only Local.

EXPECTS A COUNTER-MOVE

Kerensky, with Conservatives and Perhaps the Army Behind Him, May Save the Country.

DARK DAYS SEEN AHEAD

And Allied War Conference Faces Another Huge Problem —Bigger Burden for Us.

Reserves Cited as Showing Greater Need Than Ever For Unified Direction of Allied War Policy

By CHARLES H. GRASTY.

CADORNA IS OUTFLANKED

A General Among the Troops Cut Off on the Middle Tagliamento.

INVADERS CAPTURE 80 GUNS

Berlin Reckons Total at More Than 2,300; That of Prisoners Over 250,000.

ROME ADMITS WITHDRAWAL

Official Report Shows That Rearguard Actions Are Proceeding West of the Livenza.

British Government Denies Lack of Concern for Italy

LONDON HAILS OUR WAR MISSION

Comes at Critical Period of the

STOCKS TUMBLE ON RUSSIAN NEWS

Flood of Liquidation Hits Extion of Short Sellers.

HOPE STRONG MAN WILL RULE RUSSIA

Zemstvos' Agent Here and Herman Bernstein Agree That Kerensky Must Go.

THREAT OF DICTATOR IN GERMAN SNARL

Government Attempts to Force Dropping of Demand for Radical Vice Chancellor.

HERTLING DENIES PROMISES

Opposition to Attack Chancellor as Soon as Reichstag Meets Unless He Yields.

Insists Emperor Charles Will Be Polish Ruler

Headlines from the *New York Times,* November 9, 1917.
© 1917 by the New York Times Company. Reprinted by permission.

leaders in history have been. A strange popular leader—a leader purely by virtue of intellect; colourless, humourless, uncompromising and detached, without picturesque idiosyncrasies— but with the power of explaining profound ideas in simple terms, of analysing a concrete situation. And combined with shrewdness, the greatest intellectual audacity. . . .

Now Lenin, gripping the edge of the reading stand, letting his little winking eyes travel over the crowd as he stood there waiting, apparently oblivious to the long-rolling ovation, which lasted several minutes. When it finished, he said simply, "We shall now proceed to construct the Socialist order." Again that overwhelming human roar.*

Lenin spoke of peace: "The question of War and Peace is so clear that I think that I may, without preamble, read the project of a Proclamation to the Peoples of All the Belligerent Countries."
Reed said,

His great mouth, seeming to smile, opened wide as he spoke; his voice was hoarse—not unpleasantly so, but as if it had hardened that way after years and years of speaking—and went on monotonously, with the effect of being able to go on forever. . . . No gestures. And before him, a thousand simple faces looking up in intent adoration.†

Trotsky recorded the scene, too:

And the eyes of many rested on the short, sturdy figure of the man . . . with his extraordinary head, his high cheekbones and simple features, altered now by the shaved beard, and with that gaze of his small, slightly Mongol eyes which looked straight through everything. . . . He was not a myth. There he stood among his own. . . . Even those nearest, those who knew well his place in the party, for the first time fully realized what he meant

* Reed, *Ten Days that Shook the World,* p. 125.
† *Ibid.,* p. 127.

to the revolution, to the people, to the peoples. It was he who had taught them; it was he who had brought them up.*

Lenin was reiterating his stand: no annexations or indemnities, self-determination for various countries and national groups, publication and repudiation of secret treaties, an immediate armistice. There was little discussion; at 10:35 the vote was taken. "One delegate dared to raise his hand against, but the sudden sharp outburst around him brought it swiftly down. . . . Unanimous." Reed said,

> Suddenly, by common impulse, we found ourselves on our feet, mumbling together into the smooth lifting unison of the *Internationale*. A grizzled old soldier was sobbing like a child. . . . The immense sound rolled through the hall, burst windows and doors and seared into the quiet sky. "The war is ended! The war is ended!" said a young workman near me, his face shining.†
> Then, in the hush that followed, someone shouted, "Comrades! Let us remember those who have died for liberty!" So we began to sing the Funeral March, that slow melancholy and yet triumphant chant, so Russian and so moving. . . the very soul of those dark masses whose delegates sat in this hall, building from their obscure visions a new Russia—and perhaps more.‡

But the Bolsheviks' fight was far from over. Moscow still had eight bloody days to live through before there was even initial victory there, and the provinces had hardly grasped what was happening. Even within Petrograd there were strikes of skilled workers and professionals. (Officials of the old governnment hid or destroyed their records and refused to show the Bolsheviks their routines.) There was still an international war, and there was very nearly national anarchy. There was the promised Constituent Assembly, so soon to show the gap between Bolshevik preaching and Bolshevik practice. There were obstacles

---

* Trotsky, *History of the Russian Revolution,* 3:328.
† Reed, *Ten Days that Shook the World,* p. 132.
‡ *Ibid.*

which seemed insurmountable, to be worked out in a climate evolved from hundreds of years of misrule, in a country where the majority of people were illiterate. The peasantry would have to be dragged into the twentieth century, fighting all the way. There was the problem of minorities, most of them fiercely proud of their individual heritages. (Lenin estimated that 57 percent of the population were members of minority groups. There were more than 100 such groups, and more nearly 200 languages and dialects.) But Lenin had foreseen these problems; he had said, "If Socialism can only be realized when the intellectual development of all the people permits it, then we shall not see Socialism for at least five hundred years." It was his readiness to assume these burdens and to push through programs to deal with them that made Lenin indispensible to the Bolshevik government.

The revolution could not have happened without Lenin. He had arrived in the nick of time—if the Social Democrats had reunited and supported the Provisional Government, as they were clearly planning to do, there would have been no revolution. And if Lenin had not had the dogged, almost monomaniacal determination to move the Bolsheviks in his direction, to refuse to allow them to falter or turn aside, there still would have been no revolution. And if he had not insisted that they get on with it, there would have been no revolution. Trotsky wrote,

> If we had not seized power in October, we would not have seized it at all. Our strength . . . lay in . . . the masses, who believed that this party would do what the others had not done. If they had seen any vacillation . . . they would have drifted away from us as they did formerly from the Socialist Revolutionaries and the Mensheviki. The bourgeoisie would have had a breathing space and would have made use of it to conclude peace. . . . [This was the cause of Lenin's] uneasiness, his anxiety, his mistrust and his ceaseless hurry, that saved the revolution.*

* Leon Trotsky, *Lenin* (New York: Minton, Balch and Co., 1925), p. 87.

Although the name did not become official until March 8, 1918, the Communist regime had begun. Lenin began it and Lenin made it viable. There have been many men in history capable of making revolutions, but very few capable of directing a working administration afterward. In a country hungry, exhausted, impoverished, demoralized, backward, and still at war, Lenin's administrative genius won out over all obstacles, including those within his own party. (Within days of the insurrection, 5 out of 22 members of the Bolshevik Central Committee, and five major commissars, had resigned their posts and begun an intraparty fight against Lenin.)

From 1918 on, Lenin was a dictator.* He was not autocratic by nature, which was Russia's good fortune; after centuries of autocracy, the people could not do without it, and craved an absolute dictator. They cast Lenin in the role of protector and savior, as they once had pictured the tsar. When programs went wrong they blamed "them," never him. He was indifferent to their adulation except when he could use it to further Communist programs, and totally uninterested in personal power, pomp, or ceremony. He lived as simply in the Kremlin as he had lived in the succession of rented rooms all over Europe.

Lenin ruled by persuasion rather than by terror. He was apt to send loyal but disruptive Communists on diplomatic missions that kept them traveling and out of domestic politics, rather than to Siberia or to jail. And if he later became ruthless in weeding out party enemies, it was always in the cause of Communism, never from personal ambition or from fear, as in Stalin's case. He served Communism as a devout priest might serve his religion—as kindly as possible, but with the convic-

---

* Theoretically, the executive committee of the Soviet could have dismissed him from the chairmanship of the Council of Commissars, or the party congress could have failed to elect him to the Central Committee, in which case he would have lost his leadership, but considering his place in the Russian scene, such action would have been fantastic.

Lenin's room in the house in Simbirsk (now called Ulyanovsk).
This is now a museum; the little sign on the wall at the upper
left says "Vladimir's room." Courtesy Sovfoto.

tion that when individual and dogma clash, the individual must
either be convinced of his folly or expelled from the group.

Lenin changed the course of history, and today one-third of
the world's population lives in Communist countries. Moreover,
no matter how they interpret his teachings or quarrel among
themselves—for nationalism is still stronger than any political
"ism" in the world—Lenin is each country's hero. Maxim
Gorky, the Russian writer, said, "Lenin was a man who prevented people from leading their accustomed lives as no one
before him was able to do." The echoes of his voice are still
reverberating around the world.

Suggested Reading

To understand revolutionary Russia it is necessary to read many authors. Books by eyewitnesses such as Trotsky naturally are very important, but since they are often highly partisan, it is best to read them after you have a sufficient grasp of events to make your own judgment. Russian history has many competent interpreters who do not always agree. Ultimately each reader must make up his own mind as to what be believes, and the more he reads, the better he is able to decide. Here are some good books to start with:

CHAMBERLIN, WILLIAM HENRY. *The Russian Revolution, 1917–1921.* 2 vols. New York: Grosset, 1935. The hardbound edition is out of print, but the book is available in paperback: Grosset, Universal Library, 1965.

   Chamberlin was the *Christian Science Monitor's* Moscow correspondent from 1922 to 1934. During those years he interviewed people, examined and recorded documents, and amassed the information packed into this book. It was the first comprehensive study of the revolution to be published in the United States and is still a very valuable introduction.

FISCHER, LOUIS. *The Life of Lenin.* New York: Harper, 1964. Paperback edition: Harper Colophon Books, 1965.

   Professor Fischer first visited Russia in 1922. He met Lenin and talked with many persons who had taken part in the October Revolution. This book reflects more than 30 years of familiarity with the Soviet scene and is one of the best biographies of Lenin. It presupposes familiarity with the background and so may demand special application, but it is crammed with authoritative information, especially on the years following the October Revolution.

REED, JOHN. *Ten Days That Shook the World.* New York: Random House, Modern Library, 1960, paperback editions: International Publishers Co., 1967; New York: Signet Books, New York: Vintage Books.

John Reed was an American journalist sent to Russia to report on the revolution. Young and idealistic, his reaction to the obvious sufferings of the poor and the indifference of the rich was to fall in love with the revolution. He rushed about asking questions and squirreling documents—he pocketed everything from a poster extolling cleanliness at Smolny to the doodles left in the Winter Palace by a minister—and recorded everything in his book. It is more a valentine than an objective account, but it has an excitement and enthusiasm that brings events to life. Later Reed became disenchanted with the Communist regime and might have written quite differently, but he died of typhus in Moscow in 1920 at the age of 32. He was given a state funeral and his ashes are interred in the Kremlin Wall.

TROTSKY, LEON. *The History of the Russian Revolution.* Translated from the Russian by Max Eastman. Ann Arbor: University of Michigan Press, 1957; paperback edition: Garden City: Doubleday Anchor Books, 1959.

Naturally this is a subjective account. It was written after Trotsky had been ousted by Stalin, and Trotsky was intent on justifying his past, identifying his aims with those of Lenin, and reminding everyone of his importance to the revolution. But he *was* indispensable to the revolution and his account has the authority and detail that could only have been supplied by one of the men who made it happen.

ULAM, ADAM. *The Bolsheviks.* New York: Macmillan, 1955; paperback edition: New York: Collier Macmillan, 1968.

The Bolshevik party, from its beginnings to Lenin's death in

1924, with Lenin always at the center of the stage. Although long and necessarily complicated, this book makes a good introduction because it supplies background and identifies people and places as they are first mentioned.

BIBLIOGRAPHY

These are the sources quoted in the text:

KRUPSKAYA, NADEZHDA KONSTANTINOVNA. *Reminiscences of Lenin.* Translated by Bernard Isaacs. Moscow: Foreign Languages Publishing House, 1959.

LENIN, VLADIMIR ILYICH. *Collected Works.* 38 vols. Moscow: Foreign Languages Publishing House, 1941–1958.

————. *Lenin o Mezhdunarodnoi Politike i Mezhdunarodnom Prave.* [Lenin on International Policy and International Law]. Moscow: Institute of International Relations, 1958.

REED, JOHN. *Ten Days That Shook the World.* New York: Boni and Liveright, 1919.

SHULGIN, VASILII V. *Dni* [Days]. Leningrad, 1927.

SUKHANOV, N. N. *Zapiski o Revoliutsii* [Notes on the Revolution]. 7 vols. Berlin, Petersburg, and Moscow: Z. J. Grschebin, 1922.

TROTSKY, LEON. *The History of the Russian Revolution.* 3 vols. Translated from the Russian by Max Eastman. New York: Simon and Schuster, 1932.

————. *Lenin.* New York: Minton, Balch and Co., 1925.

Index

147